ITALY

A CONCISE HISTORY OF

ITALY

by Vincent Cronin

Published by
AMERICAN HERITAGE PUBLISHING CO., INC.
CASSELL · LONDON

CASSELL & COMPANY LTD
35 Red Lion Square, London WCIR 4SJ
Sydney, Auckland, Toronto, Johannesburg

First published in Great Britain 1973
(I.S.B.N. 0 304 29236 2)
Manufactured in the United States of America

	MAP	2
I	ROME AND THE MAKING OF ITALY	6
II	FROM REPUBLIC TO PRINCIPATE	30
III	THE EMPIRE AND ITS DECLINE	46
IV	THE DARK AGES	70
V	RISE OF THE CITY-STATES	86
VI	THE EARLY RENAISSANCE	106
VII	THE LATER RENAISSANCE	128
VIII	DECADENCE	154
IX	THE REMAKING OF ITALY	172
X	MODERN ITALY	198
	CHRONOLOGY	218
	CREDITS AND INDEX	220

CHAPTER I

ROME AND
THE MAKING OF
ITALY

The land of Italy is a long, narrow, mountainous peninsula thrusting diagonally from the Alps deep into the Mediterranean. Its length is about 750 miles; its coastline, including the islands of Sicily and Sardinia, is 5,300 miles; and its area measures almost 120,000 square miles. The land, which possesses a definite geographical unity, occupies a central position within the Mediterranean, the southern coast of Sicily being only ninety miles from Africa, and the heel of Italy the same distance from Greece. Italy is clearly well placed to receive influences from all the lands bordering the Mediterranean and, should its people be sufficiently strong, to dominate those lands either politically or commercially.

Italy's land frontier lies along the line of the Alps. Because of its great length—about 1,250 miles—the frontier is not easily defended. Moreover, many passes render the Alps more a bridge than a barrier. Italy, therefore, possesses, as well as its many potential sea links, good land links with France, the German-speaking countries, and, via Slovenia, the Balkans.

The land is not naturally rich. It possesses few metals, little coal or

This Etruscan funerary urn is shaped to resemble a mud-and-thatch hut of the Villanovan culture (1000 to 750 B.C.).

petroleum. Four-fifths is mountainous or hilly, so that crops can be grown only in the rare plainland, or on terraced fields laboriously cut and maintained on the hillsides. Internal communication is rendered difficult by the buttresses of the Apennines, Italy's main spinal ridge, and by the absence of any important river save the Po. The climate, which non-Italians think of as idyllic, is in fact composed of extremes. Lombardy is cool and damp, and Milan gets as much fog as San Francisco; high towns in the Apennines experience bitter, snowbound winters, while southern Sicily is often swept by desiccating siroccos that blow from the African deserts. But the climate, though rigorous, is not such as to make cultivation impossible, and with effort, the land can be made to produce corn and rice, fruit, olives, and wine grapes of high quality. Originally, the mountains were covered with thick forest, of which little now remains. The coastal seas were until recently well stocked with fish ranging in size from sardine to tuna, and have proved an important source of food.

The earliest inhabitants of whom we have evidence are cave dwellers of the paleolithic age (about 10,000 B.C.), who have left bone implements, graffiti, and rock paintings inferior in quality to the cave paintings of southern France and Spain. In the Neolithic Age there are signs of pastoral life and the making of pottery; in the late Copper Age (c. 2500 B.C.) painted pottery and articles of copper begin to appear. Cave dwellings are replaced by huts grouped in villages enclosed within stone walls or in natural defensive positions. There is a remarkable variety of buildings reflecting a diversity of tribes. In Apulia the dead were buried in megalithic tombs, while in Sardinia early peoples constructed the peculiar *nuraghi*—fortress-towers in the shape of a truncated cone with a domed roof; in northern Italy houses were often built on piles on the edge of a lake.

The first inhabitants of Italy of whom we have close knowledge are the Etruscans, who probably landed on the shores of what is now Tuscany between the tenth and eighth centuries B.C. They came from the eastern Mediterranean: according to Herodotus, from Lydia in Asia Minor. They were a town-dwelling people, in contrast to the people they found when they landed, who still clung to village life. The Etruscans built towns high in the mountains of Tuscany, inland at Orvieto and Chiusi, and later at Volterra, Perugia, and Arezzo. This part of Italy possesses minerals. There were copper mines between Populonia and Volterra; tin, lead, and zinc were also mined there. The Etruscans used bronze extensively and early developed an export trade in bronze figurines. They were also clever builders. They used arches and barrel vaulting, and they provided their houses with water pipes, fountains, and sewers. Some of their streets were fifty feet wide and paved with pebbles. Each town was ruled by a king, who went attended by lictors bearing the fasces, a tied bundle of rods and an axe, signifying his power of chastisement and execution.

Etruscan writing, which used a Greek alphabet, is known to us through many inscriptions. These we can read and pronounce, but the clicks and hisses which were characteristic of spoken Etruscan have not yet been deciphered. It is likely, however, that many deal with augury and religion, for from other evidence the Etruscans are known to have been religious-minded, and the only Etruscan books the Romans translated were the *Disciplina Etrusca,* volumes of religious lore. The Etruscans took omens chiefly from thunderbolts and the livers of sacrificial victims, which were read by specially trained diviners.

Etruscan men wore a short tunic and a cloak; their women, a long shift and pointed shoes. The women were treated with a consideration unusual at that time, and were allowed to be present at social functions on equal terms with the men. A scene popular among ancient sculptors shows a couple reclining on a couch, the man's arm around his wife.

In the seventh century B.C. the Etruscans began to expand southward. They occupied first Latium, then Campania, where they founded the city of Capua and came into contact with the other important civilized communities of Italy—colonies founded by various Greek city-states. The northernmost of these Greek-speaking cities was Cumae, on the coast near Naples. Here, and in other Greek colonies, civilization was more advanced than in Tuscany. Tarentum and Paestum possessed fine temples; Pythagoras the philosopher and mathematician had settled in Crotona, while later, in the Sicilian town of Agrigentum, Empedocles evolved his theory that all things are composed of earth, fire, air, and water. But each Greek colony was out for itself, and the Greek foundations in Italy never exerted as much power as the Etruscan towns, which succeeded in banding together in strong federations.

In another part of Italy there was growing up, on the Tiber River, a settlement of Latin people which was eventually to eclipse both the Etruscan towns and the Greek colonies. The earliest settlers were attracted by the defensive value of the seven hills of what was later to become Rome. There was a settlement on the Palatine hill not long before the end of the second millennium B.C., and by 800 there were younger communities on the outer hills. The story that the town of Rome was founded by Romulus and Remus is not heard of before the end of the fourth century, and the date of Rome's foundation—753 B.C.—is also legendary. What is certain is that the town was first ruled by a king. Probably the king's power was derived from the expressed will of the community, and it is noteworthy that the succession did not pass from father to son. The king exercised supreme command both in war and in the administration of justice: he proclaimed the festivals to be observed and offered sacrifices.

In Rome the earliest political grouping of which we can be sure is the *curia,* a group of households formed for the purpose of political organization. Meeting in a *comitia* as the assembly of the Roman people, the *curiae* conferred upon the king the *imperium.* The most important of these early kings is the second, Numa Pompilius. He was renowned for his wisdom and his piety, and it was generally believed that he had derived his knowledge from Pythagoras. Numa reigned some forty years and was revered by the Romans as the author of their whole religious ritual. He built the Regia, the palace of the *pontifex maximus,* or the chief priest, and may have revised the calendar, adding two months to the ten which had formerly comprised the Roman year.

Sometime about 550 B.C. the king of the Etruscan town of Tarquinii cast covetous eyes on Rome, which was now economically important, since it controlled the salt route which crossed the Tiber at this point. The king and his army conquered Rome and introduced Etruscan ways, including military techniques, weapons, alphabet, and language.

The seventh king of Rome, the half-Etruscan, half-Greek Tarquinius Superbus, behaved tyrannically and was banished by the people. About 508 he persuaded Lars Porsena, Etruscan king of Clusium, to muster a huge army and march on Rome. According to an early tradition, a young Roman, by name Gaius Mucius, resolved to deliver his country by murdering the invading king. He went to the Etruscan camp, but by mistake killed the royal secretary. Seized and threatened with torture,

This sixth-century-B.C. sarcophagus, found at Cerveteri in Tuscany, depicts an affectionate married couple reclining together.

he thrust his right hand into the fire on the altar, and there let it burn, to show how little he minded pain. Astonished at his courage, Porsena told him to return home; and Scaevola (from *scaeva,* meaning left hand), as he was thenceforth called, urged him, out of gratitude, to make peace with Rome, since three hundred noble youths had sworn to take the king's life, and he was the first upon whom the lot had fallen. Porsena thereupon made peace with the Romans.

True or only partly true, this story symbolizes the determined fashion in which the Romans threw off Etruscan rule. Shortly afterward, with the help of the Greek colony, Cumae, they defeated the Etruscans at Aricia and consolidated their independence. The monarchy in Rome then became a republic. The king's office was thenceforth fulfilled by two men elected annually. Known as consuls, they led the armies in the field and presided over political proceedings.

At this period the territory ruled by the Romans consisted of about 350 square miles. It had few natural resources except building stone, and agriculture was the basis of livelihood. We know that lists of the consuls were kept, since the years were counted by their terms of office, and the *pontifex maximus* set down brief notes on the occasion of public sacrifices (for eclipses, bad harvests, victories, defeats, pestilences, and so forth). Treaties were inscribed, sometimes on a wooden shield covered in oxhide, and kept in a temple on the Capitoline hill.

Probably the only recognized holder of rights was the *pater,* or more fully, *paterfamilias.* The members of his family could not own property or sue or be sued in the courts. His wife was said to be "under his hand," his slaves were in his *dominium,* and he possessed the *patria potestas,* which refers to the father's authority over his descendants, including the "right of life and death." This right, though rarely exercised in historical times, was never extinguished by law. The *paterfamilias* was a priest in his own house and conducted family rites. It is an unusual feature of Roman society that it never possessed a priestly caste, excluded from secular activities, but claiming authority over the conscience and conduct of the individual. The state priests, for example, could also hold the highest civil office. One result of this system was that the gods came to be looked on chiefly as protectors of the state.

So far most of the activity in Italy had involved indigenous tribes and settlers from elsewhere in the Mediterranean. But in 390 B.C. there

The interiors of Etruscan tombs, such as this at Cerveteri, include such details as stucco reliefs of household utensils decorating the walls.

occurred the first of many invasions by tough soldiers from the north. The invaders in question were Gauls, blue-eyed, fair-haired men from the land we now call France. They defeated the Romans on the Allia, a small river flowing into the Tiber six miles from Rome, and burned their city. The Romans were saved from final ruin either by payment of ransom, or because for some other reason the Gauls retraced their steps and settled north in the Po valley. The Romans then built the so-called Servian Wall, over seven miles long, to defend their city, and improved their military tactics. Instead of grouping soldiers in a dense block or phalanx, they strung them out in three lines which advanced in successive waves.

In 343, with this more sophisticated army, Rome began a series of wars whereby she subjugated the tribes of Latium and extended her rule to all central Italy. This task took sixty years. She then advanced south, much more rapidly, in a war that lasted only six years, to the Strait of Messina. By 264 the Roman state, with allied territory, extended from Pisa and Rimini to the toe of Italy. Formerly, the name of Italy (after a tribe, the Itali) had been applied to the extreme point of the peninsula, then to southern Italy generally; now it came to designate the whole of Roman Italy.

Not all Roman Italy was inhabited by Roman citizens. A distinction has to be made between the Roman state proper and the states allied with Rome, whose combined territories were six times more extensive. Rome had unified Italy with the javelin and sword, but she kept the land unified by a remarkable display of political acumen, moderation, and flexibility. In the past it had been customary for a powerful city to impose a humiliating tribute on her allies: Athens is an example. But Rome, with greater political tact, imposed no tribute. She allowed her allies to remain free and continue exercising local autonomy; they had only to supply troops for the defense of the federation as a whole. In peace there was a community of interests, in war the sense of fraternity which arises when men, shoulder to shoulder, fight to the death. Moreover, instead of imposing a standard treaty on all her allies, Rome drafted a special treaty for each, thus breaking up larger tribes, and allowing the continuance of religious associations and leagues which presented no political danger to her. Finally, the status of allies varied according to their degree of political maturity. The Sabines, whose

customs and language most resembled those of the Romans, were
among the first to attain the franchise, but the Etruscans, with their
alien language, were not hurried into close union.

The countryside around Rome was poor, and food early became one
of the city's problems. The most favored device for mitigating this was
to dispatch surplus population to form colonies. The method was to
confiscate, in conquered territory, a portion of arable land which was
fertile enough to attract settlers at points which needed protection and
possessed a strong site readily fortified. Rome sent out many such
colonies, from Rimini in the north to Brindisi in the south. These acted
as nuclei of the Roman tradition and Roman institutions; they played
a part also in integrating the federation and making it defensible.

Let us look at Rome about 265 B.C., the year in which the conquest
of Italy was completed. It was a walled city with perhaps somewhat
under one million inhabitants. It possessed in Elba a source of iron,
and in Tuscany sources of copper, tin, zinc, and lead; but it was not an
important commercial center, and had been slow to issue coins. In the
fifth century, fines had been levied in weights of bronze, and values
at that time were one ox=10 sheep=100 pounds bronze. From 406
B.C. the state paid the soldiers' stipends with bronze and presumably
collected taxes in bronze. This unprogressive machinery was continued
during most of the fourth century, two hundred years after the Greeks
of southern Italy had begun to coin silver. But from about 330 B.C.
Rome issued in her own mint bronze in standard pieces of one pound
and fractions thereof, and drachmas and double drachmas of silver
produced under contract by Campanian mints.

Originally the male Romans had been divided into patricians, members of distinguished families who enjoyed full political rights, and
plebeians, the common people, who enjoyed personal freedom but had
no share in the administration of the state. Over the previous two
centuries the plebeians had been struggling against the patricians for
better economic conditions and parity of political rights. These they
had now achieved. In 366 a plebeian was elected consul for the first
time, and by the Hortensian Law of 287 the deliberations of the plebeians' assembly became of equal value to those of the patricians. In
theory Rome was now a democracy, but in practice the people acqui-
esced in government by the senate. The senate's rule was efficient be-

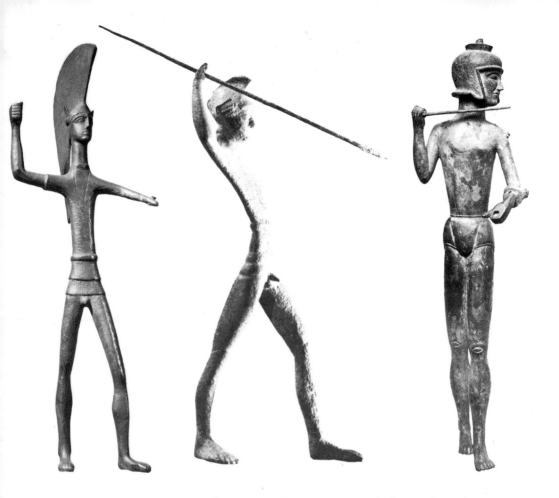

cause senators were all former magistrates, most of them talented: experienced judges, officers, and administrators, largely drawn from the wealthier families, either of patrician or plebeian origin. Rome possessed no written constitution but always held that sovereign power rested with "the senate and the Roman people."

The Romans were still a comparatively raw nation, and there was as yet no Latin literature. The earliest Roman poet, Livius Andronicus, was of Greek birth, and his first drama would be acted only in 240 B.C. On the other hand the Romans had already shown a remarkable flair for law. Their first written code, the Twelve Tables, dating from the middle of the fifth century and based on customary law, was primarily devised for an agricultural people. There is mention of the usual difficulties of the countryside—boundaries, water supply, upkeep of roads, and the like—and there are a series of enactments against damage to a

neighbor's crops by trespass, arson, or by the use of charms. Noteworthy features are that the death penalty could not be inflicted without right of appeal to the assembly and no law could be proposed against an individual.

Rome had its temples, the most important of which, on the Capitoline hill, was dedicated to three deities, Jupiter, Juno, and Minerva: a triadic arrangement borrowed from the Etruscans. The Romans tended to regard religion in legal terms. Their word for it means "binding obligation," and one of the qualities they most esteemed—*pietas*—means no more than "justice toward the gods." Their gods were abstract, utilitarian, and often personifications of moral qualities, such as Peace, Liberty, Victory, and Good Fortune. Their mythology is uninventive, and they were content to adapt Greek stories to describe events in the lives of their own deities.

Skill in warfare was essential in ancient times. Here are Etruscan warriors, a Roman war machine, and a helmet from Cumae, 474 B.C.

Perhaps the most distinctive characteristic of the early Roman is his patriotism. Many of the stories about ancient Rome concern patriots. Mucius Scaevola is one; another is Lucius Junius, the nephew of King Tarquinius. His elder brother having been murdered by Tarquinius, Lucius escaped the same fate only by feigning idiocy, whence he received the surname of Brutus. He was impelled to action against Tarquinius when one of the king's sons abducted Lucretia, the wife of one of his fellow Romans. In another typical act of patriotic heroism, she had stabbed herself rather than live in dishonor, and Brutus, seeking revenge, roused the Romans to expel the Tarquinians. Successful, he was then elected consul. Lucius Junius Brutus loved his country better than his children, for when his two sons attempted to restore the Tarquinians, in accordance with the law Brutus put them both to death.

In the coming years the Romans were to need every bit of patriotism. By unifying central and southern Italy, they had become an important Mediterranean power and soon came into collision with Carthage, across the Strait of Messina on North Africa's coast. Then the most prosperous and industrial city of the world, Carthage was both a political and trade rival. The city-state had a constitution not unlike Rome's, but with one big difference: the people of the city had no military duties. Instead, Carthage's subjects had to pay tribute, and her army was composed of conscripted subjects and hired mercenaries. She had many trading posts as far west as Cádiz in Spain; she drew tithes from more than half of Sicily; and she considered the Mediterranean her sea, where her strong navy could enforce embargo acts.

The immediate occasion of war was eastern Sicily. The town of Messina belonged to the Mamertines, a people who came originally from the Italian mainland. In 264 B.C. the Mamertines asked for admission into the Roman federation and for a protective garrison against Carthaginian encroachment. The Romans took a long time deciding. They were afraid of confronting so rich a power, but they feared also that Carthage would close the Sicilian ports to free trade and that this in time would compel their Greek allies in southern Italy, who lived by trade, to desire closer connections with Carthage in order to save their commerce with Sicily. The senate opposed the alliance, but the assembly of the people voted for it, thus precipitating the long First Punic War. Two legions were immediately sent to garrison Messina.

An Etruscan fresco c. 350 B.C. shows Charon, Lord of the Underworld.

Rome entered the war without a single battleship, while Carthage had no less than 120. These were mostly quinqueremes. Success in naval warfare depended upon driving force in ramming; three banks of oars did not provide adequate power against ships of five banks, so the senate ordered 100 quinqueremes, 150 feet long, to be built on the Punic model. Thirty thousand rowers had to be found and trained. But though they had adopted Punic-style ships, the Romans made them their own by devising a new method of naval warfare. They fitted their quinqueremes with long cranes called "ravens" that could swing grappling spikes onto the enemy's deck so as to pin the ship fast while marines boarded and cleared it.

In the first naval battle of the war, off Mylae on the northeast coast of Sicily, the new Roman fleet disposed of more than fifty ships by this method. A column was erected in the Forum to the victorious consul Duilius; it was adorned with the beaks of the conquered ships, and an inscription recorded that Duilius was the first Roman to fight on the high seas, that he captured with their crews one septereme and 30 quinqueremes and triremes, and sank many more.

In 256 the Romans decided to invade North Africa in an attempt to draw the enemy from Sicily. They fitted out 330 ships, of which perhaps 250 were battleships, and after winning a naval battle off the southern coast of Sicily, in which they captured or destroyed 80 Punic ships, they landed in Africa and occupied Tunis. But the Roman army, inefficiently led by Regulus, was defeated before Tunis by the Carthaginians, who used elephants in battle. The survivors took refuge in nearby Aspis, and there Rome sent a fleet of 350 ships to bring them back. On the homeward voyage it was wrecked in a storm off Camarina, on the Sicilian coast, and all but 80 ships were lost, together with 15 per cent of Italy's able-bodied men.

Such a disaster would have demoralized a less determined people or disrupted a less well-knit alliance, but Rome coolly raised taxes, ordered 200 new quinqueremes to be ready in three months, and somehow found 80,000 men for the naval campaign of 254 B.C., whereby she captured Panormus (Palermo), the Punic headquarters in Sicily. There followed twelve years of stalemate on land and sea. Then after a further naval victory at Drepanum (Trapani), the Romans made the Carthaginian position in Sicily untenable, and the peace was signed.

The Carthaginians were to evacuate Sicily, to give up all prisoners without ransom, and to pay a large war indemnity.

Rome's success was remarkable proof that the federation she had formed was a viable and powerful entity. The surprise of the war was that the Romans, who knew nothing of seamanship before it, won six of the seven naval battles. No great generals had emerged, but what the consuls lacked in experience they had made up for by determination. The most important result of the war was that Italy now decided to become a tribute-imposing nation, like Carthage. Tribute of 10 per cent on crops was imposed on about half the island of Sicily. This was Rome's first step in the formation of a tribute-paying empire.

The other important result was to make Italy a naval power. Thenceforth, the northern Mediterranean was her sea, not Carthage's. Sardinia, formerly a Carthaginian colony, was occupied by Rome in 238, and Corsica slightly later. In 227 the two islands were made into a province like Sicily, and tithes were thenceforth collected.

The Second Punic War began in 218, and this time Rome had a much more difficult struggle, nearer home. The brilliant young Carthaginian general, Hannibal, set out from Carthago Nova, his base in southern Spain, crossed the Pyrenees, then Gaul, and finally led his

In legend, the abandoned twins Remus and Romulus were suckled by a wolf. Later Romulus killed Remus in a dispute over the founding of Rome.

army, which included elephants, over the Alps, probably using the pass known today as the Little Saint Bernard. Entering northern Italy, he twice defeated a Roman army. In 217, after wintering among the Gaulish tribes, Hannibal marched into Tuscany through the marshes along the banks of the Arno River. In struggling through these marshes his army suffered severely, and he himself contracted ophthalmia, losing the sight of one eye. The consul Flaminius hastened to meet him, and a battle was fought at Lake Trasimeno, in which the Roman army was destroyed, and the consul killed. The following year a Roman army of perhaps 12,000 (Polybius claimed it was closer to 90,000) was annihilated at Cannae. This defeat was followed by the revolt from Rome of most of her allies in southern Italy.

Rome was on the brink of despair. Historians told that the very gods began to tremble; their statues sweated blood, and two-headed lambs were born with alarming frequency. The plebeians and patricians had for centuries been locked in rivalry; had either group sided with the invader posterity would have heard no more of the Roman state. But in this ultimate crisis the Romans gave further proof of their remarkable patriotism. They closed ranks, put 200,000 men under arms, harried Hannibal, who had established himself in Capua, and defeated his brother Hasdrubal at the head of a relief army. The first news of that battle came to Hannibal when the Romans tossed over the rampart into his camp the bleeding head of his defeated brother. Finally, in 203, the Romans compelled Hannibal to return to Africa. There he was pursued and defeated, as a result of which in 201 Carthage made peace. Rome became mistress of the entire western Mediterranean.

The whole of southern Italy suffered terribly from devastation in this war. Some four hundred villages were wiped out. The use of slaves also increased rapidly during the war, as there was a shortage of manpower. No fewer than 30,000 people were captured by the Romans in Tarentum in 209 and sold into slavery.

What were the Romans like at this period? We get a glimpse of their strong community spirit in the career of Lucius Caecilius Metellus, who held the offices of consul and *pontifex maximus*. Metellus captured sixty elephants in the First Punic War and, in rescuing the Palladium (the sacred statue of Pallas, on whom the safety of the city was thought to depend) when the temple of Vesta was on fire, lost the sight of both eyes. When the consul died in 221, his son in a funeral oration spoke of his father's ideals, saying that he had striven for the highest offices of state, for wealth honorably attained, for the respect of the community won by acts of courage and counsels of wisdom, and that he had desired a family of many children to survive him.

A more detailed portrait can be drawn of a second Roman: the leading general during the Second Punic War. Publius Cornelius Scipio was born in 234. His family was one of the five great families of Rome, and three generations of Scipios had held the consulship. A portrait bust shows Scipio to have been handsome, with fleshy cheeks, large almost visionary eyes, and a determined mouth. Before embarking upon any expedition he always went to the temple to pray. There was a belief that he was a special favorite of Heaven and held communication with the gods. It is possible that he shared this belief; it would help account for his immense self-confidence and powers of leadership.

Scipio was a precocious soldier. At sixteen he saved his father's life on the battlefield, and at eighteen fought at Cannae, being one of the few Roman officers to survive that disaster. Afterward he made the Roman patricians who had thought of leaving Italy in despair swear on oath with drawn sword to continue the struggle.

At twenty-four Scipio was given the command in Spain. There he made a favorable impression by his kindly treatment of Spanish prisoners: he sent back a daughter to her father and a wife to her husband. At the battle of Baecula he defeated Hannibal and drove the Carthaginians out of Spain. Three times in Spain, it is said, Scipio declined the title of King; Romans were proud of their republican government and disapproved of kingship, which they identified with the tyranny of Tarquinius. Scipio returned to Rome in 206, and though he had not held the prerequisite office of praetor, he was elected consul. He had already shown a taste for Greek culture—he wrote and spoke Greek perfectly—and this made him enemies among the old-fashioned aristocracy. The outward-looking Scipio saw Italy as a great Mediterranean power and wished to carry the war into Africa. The conservatives under Quintus Fabius Cunctator opposed this scheme, and Scipio was merely given the province of Sicily, with permission to cross to Africa if it appeared in the interests of Rome.

OVERLEAF: *The Palatine hill is the site of the original Roman settlement.*

Scipio wintered in Syracuse, finding the Greek atmosphere congenial. He walked about the gymnasium in Greek cloak and slippers, and spent his time among rhetoricians and athletes. In the spring, having offered prayer for success, Scipio sailed with 35,000 men to Africa. His first year there he acted cautiously, beating all the forces sent against him, winning certain towns, and persuading the Numidian Berbers to the Roman cause. But the following spring, learning that the Carthaginian camps were made of nothing more than branches and reeds, he reorganized his army and set the camps on fire, killing many of their troops. After further successes, he offered peace terms remarkable for their moderation. When these were rejected, he attacked Hannibal at Zama, some eighty miles southwest of Carthage, killing or wounding 20,000 Carthaginians with a loss of only 1,500 Romans. The Roman aristocracy wanted a vindictive peace settlement, but Scipio again imposed moderate terms. One of the articles, however, laid down that the Carthaginians should surrender all their warships and elephants. Scipio then returned to Rome, where he celebrated the most brilliant triumph that had yet been witnessed: he was allowed to add to his name the title of the land he had conquered—Africanus.

Idolized by his soldiers, Scipio was now one of the most powerful men in Rome. But the time had not yet come when the individual could challenge the senate's power. Scipio offered no threat to the nobility except through the normal channels of political life, in which he showed no particular ability. However, many Romans were jealous of his fame. In 185 he was accused of having misappropriated money while serving as legate in a war against the king of Syria. When the trial came, and Scipio was summoned, he proudly reminded the people that this was the anniversary of the day on which he had defeated Hannibal at Zama, and called upon them to follow him to the Capitol, in order there to return thanks to the immortal gods, and to pray that they would send other citizens like himself. This was the kind of grandiloquent gesture which appealed to the Romans, and he was followed by crowds to the Capitol; the charge against him was allowed to lapse.

Scipio retired to his country estate at Liternum on the coast of Campania. Here, living in comparative poverty, he wrote his memoirs in Greek. He had married Aemilia, daughter of Aemilius Paulus, who had been killed at Cannae, and by her had two sons and two daughters,

Scipio Africanus, adversary of Cato and victor in the Second Punic War

one of whom, Cornelia, was a remarkable woman. Like her father Cornelia shared a taste for Greek literature, and was esteemed as a letter writer by Cicero. She became the mother of Tiberius and Gaius Gracchus, who were to play as important a part in Italian domestic politics as their grandfather had played in the Second Punic War.

Scipio is typical of the best Italians of the early republic. A good family man, with strong public spirit, he lived frugally and showed a remarkable moderation in his dealings with other states. He was gracious and sympathetic to those around him but, we are told, harsh and arrogant to his political enemies, and in this, prefigured the spirit of faction and party warfare which were later to damage Rome. He was a religious man, but no narrow sectarian: he dedicated votive offerings to Apollo at Delos and Delphi, and it was under his consulship that the cult of Cybele, the Great Mother Goddess, was transferred from Phrygia to Rome. Above all, Scipio was a patriot who served his country ably in a desperate war by that rare blend of caution and daring which makes for continued success in the field.

The end of the Second Punic War marks the emergence of the Roman federation of Italy as the dominant power in the Mediterranean. Three hundred years earlier Rome had been a small riverside community of little importance. She had expanded steadily through war: no people in antiquity showed greater stamina in war over a period of many generations. The Romans, unquestionably, were sturdy, patriotic, and brave, but the unique thing about them is that they combined these qualities with political acumen and rare good sense. By treating the peoples they conquered moderately and with tact they were able to win them over, and eventually to civilize them. That, in a wider context, was to be the next phase of the Roman achievement.

A Spanish manuscript of the fifteenth century illustrates Hannibal crossing the Alps to attack Rome in 218 B.C.

CHAPTER II

FROM REPUBLIC
TO PRINCIPATE

F or three centuries Italy had been the scene of wars. At last, with
the beginning of the second century B.C., a lull came, and a period of
prosperity. This coincided with the final submission in 191 of northern Italy, known from its Gaulish inhabitants as Cisalpine Gaul, so
that now the whole peninsula we know today as Italy came under the
rule of Rome.

During the second century the Roman legions fought and conquered abroad, wherever Italy's position as a great Mediterranean
power demanded it. Between 197 and 133 most of Spain was brought
under Roman rule, in 146 most of Greece, and in 121 southern France
became the province of Gallia Narbonensis, a status still reflected in
its present-day name of Provence. This growth of empire increased
the prosperity of Italians, who found a wider market for their chief
products, wine and oil. At the same time they became accustomed to
ideas and values of the countries they ruled, and evolved a remarkable
toleration of them. Whereas the Greeks had been in many respects
proud and introverted, with scarcely a good word to say for the
barbarians who could not speak Greek, the Italians at this stage treated

*The small compartments under the arena in which waiting gladiators and wild
animals were kept are visible in the excavations of the Colosseum.*

provincials if not quite as equals at least with interest, and were prepared to learn from them. For example, from 200 B.C., well-to-do Italians went to Greece for their higher education. Cicero, Caesar, and Horace traveled to Athens or Rhodes, and they spoke and wrote Greek as fluently as Latin.

Now that Italy was a unified and peaceful whole, the other Italians pressed Rome to grant them citizenship. The Romans were reluctant to extend this privilege and the outsiders, in 91 B.C., had to go to war —the so-called Social War—to secure what they wanted. In a series of measures beginning 89 B.C. all Italians were given citizenship. The new citizens, most of them living far from Rome, were unable to attend the assemblies in that city—there was as yet no notion of representative government—and so they were still excluded from the exercise of power on a national scale. However, all towns now received a form of municipal constitution, with senate, assembly, and four chief magistrates, two for the administration of justice, two for the supervision of municipal interests. As Roman citizens the Italians were exempt from taxes, but with their strong civic sense they vied with each other to endow their towns with fine buildings: schools, libraries, baths, orphanages. This was the beginning of a strong municipal spirit which would last into the Middle Ages and is still alive today.

In Rome on the other hand political life was less healthy. It had always been a weakness of the constitution that the plebeians had no means of articulating their wishes. They might deliberate on measures proposed by the senate, and vote yes or no, but they might not initiate legislation. Since many thousands led a life of idleness, supported by the *annona,* or public dole of wheat, or as "hangers on" of millionaire citizens, they had time to brood on their discontent and to support any leader who promised them better conditions or more political power.

The first of these ambitious popular leaders was Tiberius Gracchus, grandson of Scipio Africanus. He was a brilliant horseman and was trained in the fine points of Greek oratory; but he also had a strong sympathy with the underdog. He believed that Italy's huge estates composed of conquered land and worked by foreign slaves for absentee landlords, were harmful to the republic as a whole. He realized that the senate, which was reactionary and full of landlords or their friends, would never reform this situation, so in 133 B.C. he had himself elected one of Rome's ten tribunes. Magistrates empowered with the veto against decisions of the senate, they were the guardians of Roman citizenry and their persons were inviolable. As tribune, Tiberius Gracchus demanded the enforcement of certain old laws, long since fallen into disuse, limiting the amount of conquered land any one man might hold. The senate, furious, put up another tribune to veto the proposals of Gracchus. Gracchus in turn declared that a tribune who opposed the people was no tribune, and had the senate's stalking horse summarily deposed. Finally an impasse was reached, and a group of senators murdered Gracchus. Ten years passed. Then Tiberius Gracchus' brother Gaius also tried to carry out agrarian and other reforms, but he too was outwitted by the senate. In a riot he and his supporters were worsted: three thousand of his party were killed and Gaius commanded his slave to put him to death.

The next leader of the people was Gaius Marius. A farmer-soldier, Marius stood for the consulship in 107, and though he lacked influential friends, was elected and given command of the army in Africa. Having won a victory there, he returned to save Italy from an invasion by Germanic peoples, the Cimbri and the Teutoni. Although the laws forbade re-election, Marius was so popular that he became consul six times and pushed through a program in opposition to the senate.

The aristocratic party was awaiting its chance to fight back and presently found a leader in Lucius Cornelius Sulla, a general at least as brilliant as Marius. After the Social War, which took place at this time, Sulla marched his army into the streets of Rome, drove out Marius, and in the year 88 was complete master of the city. He then left for the East to fight the Persian, Mithridates, king of Pontus. Marius immediately returned, butchered the leading senators, and was elected to a seventh consulship in 86. In the same year he died. Marius' seven consulships had made a mockery of republican institutions and expedited their decay.

For four years another demagogue, Lucius Cornelius Cinna, ruled as monarch at Rome. Year after year he assumed the consulship and nominated the other magistrates without the formality of election. He repealed the laws of Sulla and won the gratitude of the common people by reducing all debts by 75 per cent. Then he set out to supersede Sulla in the East, only to be murdered by his own troops.

Sulla came home in 83 at the head of five veteran legions, defeated the popular party, and was once more master of Rome. He proscribed 80 senators, 3,600 knights, and over 2,000 private citizens: all were immediately killed and their heads nailed up in the Forum. Sulla assumed the dictatorship, enacted a whole new constitution increasing the power of the senate, and then, in 79 B.C., suddenly retired from public life. He died in his bed a year later from the effects of debauchery. Hardly was his body cold than another consul had marched on Rome and the city streets were once again running with blood.

For the next thirty years Italy was to be rent by the civil wars of rival politicians, many of them generals. The period of the republic, a century later, would be idealized by historians such as Livy and Tacitus, who looked back longingly to what they believed had been idyllic days of constitutional government; but the facts are otherwise. The constitution was never adequate to Rome's needs, it was constantly being infringed, and the last century of the republic was a morass of party thuggery and bloody vendettas.

Most of the changes effected by the Gracchi, Marius, and Sulla were of short duration, but one was permanent and of immense importance. This was the creation of a professional army by Marius. The old citizen militia raised for an annual spring campaign was no longer up to the intricacies of modern war or many years' service abroad, with the result that Rome usually started a war with a series of defeats, while her raw recruits were learning their trade. Moreover, the wealthier recruits were undisciplined and sometimes mutinous.

Marius, himself of peasant origins, ended the rule whereby only men of property might join the army and opened his ranks to the poor, sturdy peasants of Italy. These formed the infantry, other arms being provided by foreign experts: cavalry from the Numidian deserts, slingers from the Balearic Islands, archers from Crete, and so on. Having thus professionalized his army, Marius abolished all distinctions in the ranks. All the men of the line had standard equipment supplied by the state and instead of a variety of insignia now fought under one emblem—the silver eagle, regarded as sacred. Legions instead of being disbanded at the close of a campaign had a permanent existence, and the numbers in each legion were raised to six thousand men.

The improved Roman legion attacked in three lines, each many

HOUSE OF VETTII, POMPEII; ALFREDO FOGLIA

ranks deep. First they threw their javelins, the heads of which were displaced if they struck an impenetrable object—Marius' own invention—so that the missiles could not immediately be hurled back by the enemy. Then the legionaries went in with short, broad swords. They wore brass helmets and protected their bodies with wooden shields. After fighting for fifteen minutes, a legionary rested while another took his place.

For attacking towns and strong villages, the Romans used the onager, a siege engine, which was powered by twisted skeins of sinew or hair and flung a flaming log or a rock missile; the crossbow-like catapult which shot arrows, pebbles, and lead shot; the balista which hurled sixty-pound stones. Hooks to pull stones from a wall, tunnels, siege towers, battering rams, and mass attacks by soldiers under cover of a "tortoise shell" of shields were the chief techniques used for capturing a stronghold.

Wheat, salt, and wine were offered in the lararium, *or household shrine.*

A professional standing army of this nature was bound to change the tenor of Roman politics. It almost immediately became a third force, stronger than either senate or popular assembly. Marius was the first Roman general who found that he could count on his soldiers to back him if necessary against the government. But he lacked the statesmanship necessary to make good use of his power. It was to be found, fifty years later, in Marius' nephew: Gaius Julius Caesar.

As a boy, Julius Caesar witnessed the horrifying excesses of Marius and Sulla, and it was then perhaps that he resolved to bring order to Roman politics. On his first campaign he saved the life of a fellow soldier, for which he was awarded the coveted honor of the civic oak-leaf crown. He was an excellent speaker and perfected his technique at Rhodes. At the age of thirty-one he entered politics as a candidate of the popular party. In order to win the people's favor he plunged deeply into debt to stage wild beast shows, theatrical performances, and gladiatorial combats. In 60 B.C. he formed a coalition, known as the triumvirate, with Pompey, an able general whose conquests in Asia Minor had almost doubled Rome's revenues, and the millionaire Crassus. Julius Caesar served as consul in 59, then obtained the governorship for five years of Cisalpine Gaul (northern Italy, recently given the new status of a province) and Transalpine Gaul (southeastern France). He had sole command of 24,000 troops, and with this army was presently to change the course of Italian history.

"Caesar," according to Suetonius, "is said to have been tall, fair, and well-built, with a rather broad face and keen, dark-brown eyes. His health was sound, apart from sudden comas and a tendency to nightmares which troubled him toward the end of his life; but he twice had epileptic fits while on campaign. He was something of a dandy, always keeping his head carefully trimmed and shaved; and has been accused of having certain other hairy parts of his body depilated with tweezers. His baldness was a disfigurement which his enemies harped upon, much to his exasperation; but he used to comb the thin strands of hair forward from his poll, and of all the honors voted him by the senate and people, none pleased him so much as the privilege of wearing a laurel wreath on all occasions—he constantly took advantage of it . . . . His affairs with women are commonly described as numerous and extravagant . . . . Yet not even his enemies denied that he drank abstemiously . . . . He was not particularly honest in money matters, either while a governor or while holding office at Rome."

As a general, Caesar's motto was *celeritas*—speed. He used to address his troops not as "My men," but as "Comrades," which they liked better. "He always led his army," Suetonius continues, "more often on foot than in the saddle, went bareheaded in sun and rain alike, and could travel for long distances at incredible speed in a gig, taking very little luggage. If he reached an unfordable river he would either swim or propel himself across it on an inflated skin . . . . Religious scruples never deterred him for a moment. At the formal sacrifice before he launched his attack on Scipio and King Juba [of Mauretania], the victim escaped; but he paid no heed to this most unlucky sign and marched off at once . . . . It was his rule never to let enemy troops rally when he had routed them, and always therefore to assault their camp at once . . . . If Caesar's troops gave ground he would often rally them in person, catching individual fugitives by the throat and forcing them round to face the enemy again . . . . While attacking a bridge at Alexandria, Caesar was forced by a sudden enemy sortie to jump into a row-boat. So many of his men followed him that he dived into the sea and swam 200 yards until he reached the nearest Caesarian ship—holding his left hand above water the whole way to keep certain documents dry; and towing his purple cloak behind him with his teeth, to save this trophy from the Egyptians."

Caesar was not by nature cruel, but he could not escape the standards of his age. He had deserters, mutineers, and sleeping sentries stoned to death, he crucified a band of pirates who had kidnapped him, and on one occasion ordered the massacre of 430,000 men, women, and children of German tribes peacefully withdrawing across the Rhine: the figure is his own.

Caesar's spectacularly successful conquest of all Gaul excited Pompey's jealousy, and Pompey persuaded the senate to order Caesar to disband his army. Two of the tribunes vetoed this decree, but the senate, illegally, refused to abide by the veto. Caesar marched south. The Rubicon (a small river flowing into the Adriatic and now designated as the Fiumicino) separated Cisalpine Gaul from Italy proper. It was illegal to lead his troops out of his own province, hence the significance in Caesar's career of "crossing the Rubicon." His march on Rome turned out to be a triumphal procession. He then pursued Pompey and crushed him at Pharsalus. In Alexandria he met and mastered Cleopatra; at Zela in Pontus he came, saw, conquered.

At the end of July, 47 B.C., Caesar returned to Rome undisputed master of the Roman world. Unlike other conquerors in civil wars, he forgave all who had fought him, and sought to win over the senate by declaring that he would make no distinction between Pompeians and Caesarians. In 46 he reformed the calendar, replacing the old year of 355 days with a new one of 365 days: an action which excited distrust among extreme republicans, since it was King Numa who had last altered the calendar, and kings were detested in Rome. A further campaign in Spain, during which he crushed Pompey's sons, increased Caesar's popularity with the people and his power. When tribunes opposed his wishes, he deposed them, and statues of him began to appear among those honoring the gods. He thus aroused the envy and hatred of the aristocracy. Finally, more than sixty enemies banded together and on the ides of March, 44 B.C., had Julius Caesar assassinated.

Though he died at the early age of fifty-five, Caesar had set the pat-

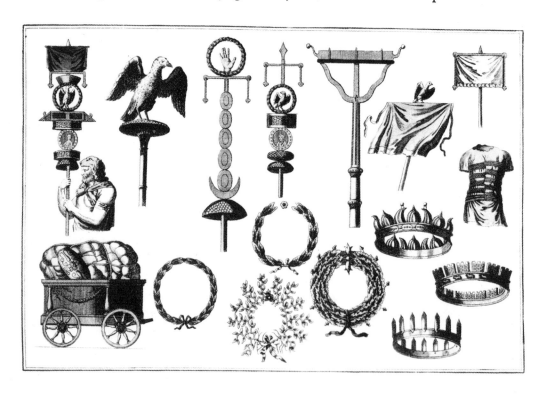

tern for a new system of government more effective than the old, whereby power was to be divided between the senate and a single man, known as the princeps, or chief citizen, representing the people's interests. After a period of civil war Caesar's adopted son, Octavian, became princeps and in 27 B.C. took the name Augustus, connoting increase, innovation, and reverence.

Augustus, a statesman not a soldier, showed great tact in the exercise of his power. Aware that Julius Caesar had fallen by infringing republican forms, the new princeps lived simply, treated the senate with respect, and never performed a function or assumed an office without assuring himself that it was within the constitution. He allowed the senate to govern most of the provinces, but kept for himself Syria, Gaul, and Spain, which were still unsettled and required soldiers. Ultimately, indeed, Augustus' power rested on the army, without which his constitutional position as princeps could have been challenged by any rich or powerful troublemaker. The twenty-three legions which with their auxiliaries and reserves formed the entire military force of Rome took their oath solely to Augustus and were with one exception stationed exclusively in his provinces; they took their orders from none but the princeps and his legates.

For the first time in 200 years Augustus closed the temple of Janus, which stood open only during war, so inaugurating the long *pax Romana* within Italy and all but the frontiers of empire. He reduced the army and spent lavishly on the rebuilding of Rome, declaring that he found it brick, and left it marble. He encouraged literature, protected Horace, Virgil, and Livy, and erected on the Palatine hill a magnificent marble temple with a public library annexed to it. He took a census of the Roman citizens, who were found to number 4,063,-000. There was scarcely a town in Italy to which he did not give some splendid building. He administered his provinces more fairly than the senate administered theirs, and ended the fiscal oppression which had been one of the chief blights of the republic.

Augustus undertook a more difficult task when he set himself to reform the morals of Roman society which, with peace and plenty, were becoming corrupt. In a series of laws the princeps clamped down on adultery, childless marriages, divorce, scandalous extravagance, and idleness. He set his wife and daughter to spinning and weaving,

A nineteenth-century French engraving shows battle standards, crowns, and other equipage of imperial Rome.

and would wear only cloaks of their making. Once when his daughter Julia built a palace for herself, Augustus had it demolished. The poet Ovid, author of *The Art of Love,* which is really a handbook to adultery, he banished to the Black Sea. In food and drink Augustus was most abstemious, often eating in a day only a slice of bread with a relish of pickled fish or dates or olives. His pleasures were simple: watching chariot races and playing knucklebones with slave boys.

Augustus reigned some forty years. His reign was considered by many to be a golden age, and so skillfully had he devised and implemented the system known as the principate that it would survive the vices and follies of his immediate successors. Suspicious Tiberius, mad Caligula, doddering Claudius, Nero the matricide, avaricious Galba, Otho the suicide, Vitellius the glutton—their vices are familiar from the perhaps exaggerated pages of Suetonius, yet the principate proved stronger than any one man, and continued strengthened rather than weakened through the first century. As the principate flourished, so new terms began to be used to designate the princeps. "Imperator," which formerly had signified any leader entrusted by the senate with military power, was now applied to the princeps exclusively as the man who ruled Rome, and we translate the word as "emperor." However, this term had not yet acquired its meaning of monarch. The princeps was sometimes also called "caesar," a word which originally designated nothing more than descent from the family of Julius Caesar and which as yet had no suggestion of absolute power. The princeps was still in law only the leading citizen and, for example, he might not raise taxes without consent of the senate. True, the senate was becoming a body of yes men, but this was not because the princeps oppressed them: on the contrary, it was because they realized that the authority of a strong princeps was needed if the faction and bloodshed of the first century B.C. were not to be repeated.

Trajan became princeps in 98 and ruled nineteen years. His reign is a high point in the history of Italy as of the empire. Italy then had a population of about twenty million, of which 1,200,000 were in Rome. The "capital of the world" was a city of magnificent buildings. The fire of 64 had given Nero his chance to rebuild half of Rome and to erect his fabulous Golden House with an artificial lake, drained fifteen years later for the site of the Colosseum. Dominating the city

was the Capitol, a square shrine atop Capitoline hill dedicated to the
trinity of Jupiter, Juno, and Minerva. Lower down stood the Forum, a paved open space, the setting for mass meetings, and nearby stood the Senate House. Trajan's column commemorating the conquest of Dacia—present-day Rumania—was erected in A.D. 113, with its long spiral of bronze bas-reliefs depicting scenes from the campaign. If we could enter the narrow streets we should see citizens in their flowing white togas, accompanied by slaves wearing bright tunics. There is no wheeled traffic, for this is forbidden during the day, but there are many people from abroad: tightly trousered Gauls, skin-clad Sarmatians, Parthians wearing conical hats. Perhaps the lictors come swinging down the hill bidding everyone make way for the litter of Trajan who is on his way to sacrifice.

A deep gulf divided rich and poor. The proletariat lived in five-story apartment blocks, without running water or sanitation, and heated by unsafe stoves, which caused one or more daily fires in the city. There was great overcrowding, and the diet of the poor was inadequate: wheat porridge with chick-peas and other vegetables. A hundred and fifty thousand Romans did not work at all. They lived on the wheat dole provided by the princeps. Those who did have jobs worked seven or less hours a day and did not work at all on half the days of the year, which were public holidays. Rome was a largely unproductive city, yet it bulged with goods imported from abroad. Silks, gold jewelry, pearls, ivory, coral, glass, amber, every kind of marble, were imported to pamper the tastes of the rich.

Roman law had become much less severe in a number of important respects. A father in practice no longer exercised the right of life and death over his children, and the old severity toward sons had been replaced by excessive indulgence. Divorce by consent of the two parties or at the wish of one was now common. Women enjoyed a fuller life, and we have examples of women practicing as physicians. Slaves—one in three of the population—were protected by new laws: they had to be treated humanely and could more easily secure their emancipation.

Under the republic parents had educated their children themselves, but now they could no longer be bothered with this task. They sent their children, in the morning only, to private elementary schools, where reading, writing, and arithmetic were taught. Only the middle

classes and aristocracy could afford for their sons the secondary education provided by grammarians and rhetoricians. Their lessons, in Latin and in Greek, were confined to effective public speaking, the key to a political or administrative career. Philosophy still remained under a ban passed by the senate in 161 B.C.; physics and metaphysics, politics and history, were likewise unknown in the school curriculum. Italian education remained consistently inferior to that of the ancient Greeks, and the people of Italy never became penetrating critics, either of philosophical theories or of their own political system. They were too content to rely on the much-vaunted *mos maiorum,* or popular custom.

In religion also there was a loosening of the purely legal and ritualistic formulae. Great ladies no longer climbed the Capitoline hill to pray to Jupiter for rain. There was increasing scepticism toward the old deities. The void was replaced by mysticism or more personal religions from the East. More and more of the leading thinkers began to feel that eternal happiness could not be bought by ritual but must be earned by personal merit. The word *salus,* which had formerly meant physical health, came to be used in a new sense of personal salvation. There were still only a few Christians in Rome at this time —all the first bishops, incidentally, were Greek-speaking, an indication of where the main strength of Christianity lay—but this new atmosphere was to prove favorable to the work of conversion.

Few Romans now served in the army, and the old warlike virtues had degenerated into vicarious enjoyment of cruel gladiatorial shows and mock sea battles. Juvenal's indictment is justified: "The people that once bestowed commands, consulships, legions, and all else, now meddles no more and longs eagerly for just two things—bread and circuses." When Titus inaugurated the Colosseum, five thousand beasts were killed within 100 days, and during one gladiatorial show lasting 117 days, 4,941 pairs of gladiators took part. Some gladiatorial combats were so arranged that none might escape alive. For example, an armed man was pitted against an unarmed man; when he had killed his victim, he in turn was disarmed and sent to be slaughtered by an armed newcomer. Also, at some shows, condemned criminals were dropped into a cage of wild beasts, to be mauled to death. The Romans gambled on the gladiatorial duels, as they did on chariot races, dice, and knucklebones.

"The Senate and the People of Rome" (SPQR) is an apt dedication for the statue of Julius Caesar which stands in the Roman Forum.

Amphitheaters were built rather than theaters for plays, and only rarely was serious drama performed. The public preferred erotic, lavishly produced musicals, their catchy tunes sung by one or more stars, and no less erotic mimes, the performers in which were permitted to appear nude. If a play called for a character to be slain by a mob, a condemned criminal took the part, and the audience watched with sadistic pleasure as the players tore him to pieces.

The Italians of this period ate a cold breakfast and took their one hot meal—the *cena*—after the bath, around two or three in the afternoon. Formerly a wife had eaten seated at her husband's feet, but now she too reclined with the men on one of the three sloping couches ranged around a square table. A cloth covered the table, but food was still eaten with the fingers, entailing frequent hand-washing. A *cena* in the strict sense comprised hors d'oeuvres, three entrées, two roasts,

A mosaic from Ostia shows an official measuring grain for the annona, *a government program to distribute low-cost supplies to the citizenry.*

and dessert. An immense variety of game, shellfish, meat, vegetables, including asparagus and truffles, fruits, nuts, and pickles was available to the gourmet. Dormice and peacocks were considered special delicacies. Wine mixed with water was served at dinner, but heavy drinking of neat wine began afterward. Some dinners and parties lasted eight hours, and were enlivened by clowns and dancing girls.

Rome was the mistress of a great Mediterranean empire, and it is there, rather than in the capital, that Roman virtues are to be sought. Already, by the beginning of the principate, Rome ruled Spain, France, Macedonia, Dalmatia, Greece, Syria, Egypt, and North Africa. Augustus added Judaea to the list of provinces; Caligula Morocco; Claudius Thrace and Britain; Trajan Dacia, Armenia, Mesopotamia, Assyria, and Arabia.

Vulgar Latin, the spoken language of the Romans, and Rome's way of life spread to many of these provinces. Gaul was becoming as civilized as Italy and many Gauls who could speak Latin received the *jus Latium,* which was almost equivalent to full citizenship. Claudius admitted the chiefs of the Aedui into the Roman senate, and part of the speech in which he did so is preserved on bronze tablets at Lyons. Even in distant Britain the benefits of Italian civilization were felt.

Whereas the republic had sucked the blood of her provinces, the principate gave more than it took. Romans cleared out the reed-choked canals in Egypt, opened other parts of North Africa to irrigation, set the savage Spaniards to mining and weaving, built aqueducts and bridges everywhere, established a postal system, and policed land and sea so effectively that a man might travel safely from York to Jerusalem, or from Trier to Cairo, with gold on his person. In Pliny's letters we can see how minute details were referred by a provincial governor to the princeps, and how conscientiously they were answered. The moderation and sense of justice which had marked the Romans' dealings with their allies in Italy now marked the Italians' dealings with the peoples of Europe, North Africa, and the Middle East.

CHAPTER III

THE EMPIRE
AND ITS DECLINE

T rajan was the last of the completely successful conquerors, and his reign marks a zenith. Trajan's successor, Hadrian, was not a soldier but an administrator, concerned not with extending but with consolidating and strengthening the frontiers. His characteristic monument is Hadrian's Wall, snaking its way nearly 75 miles across the north of England, to keep out marauding Picts and Scots. As part of his political strategy, Hadrian abandoned Trajan's acquisitions: Armenia, Mesopotamia, and Syria; and he fought only when absolutely necessary.

Born in Spain in 76 A.D., Hadrian was a highly cultivated man, with a prodigious memory and power of concentration. He could simultaneously write, dictate, and carry on a conversation with friends. He spent the greater part of his reign traveling through the provinces, often on foot: his first journey lasted five years. Everywhere he reorganized, consolidated, improved administration, and introduced humanitarian measures. He is also one of history's great builders. He gave Rome the temples dedicated to Venus and Roma, the plans of which he is said to have prepared himself; the mausoleum which forms the groundwork of the present Castel Sant' Angelo; and the Pantheon, the

The Arch of Septimius Severus, erected in A.D. 203, commemorates a victory over the Parthians by the emperor and his sons, Caracalla and Geta.

only Roman temple to have survived intact, because in early Christian times it was converted into a church. Hadrian built at Tibur (present-day Tivoli) an extensive villa, where he tried to reproduce the sites and buildings that had most impressed him on his travels, and which he embellished with fountains, statues, cypress avenues, ornamental lakes, and canals. In Athens he completed the greatest temple, the Olympieion, which had been standing half-finished for centuries, and added a new suburb, whose gate to this day bears the inscription: "This is the city of Hadrian, not of Theseus." In Egypt after his favorite, a handsome young Bithynian named Antinoüs, drowned in the Nile, Hadrian founded a city to commemorate him, Antinoopolis.

His love of beautiful things led Hadrian to climb Etna in order to see the sunrise from the summit; his love of learning, to surround himself with scholars and philosophers, with whom he discussed the knottiest questions. So much traveling at a time when belief in the ancient gods of Rome was waning led Hadrian to religious scepticism, but even this found wonderfully beautiful expression when, on his deathbed, he dictated to his soul the poem beginning, *Animula vagula, blandula*:

> *Tell me, sweet flittering soul, I pray,*
> *Guest and companion of my day,*
> *Whither away, whither away,*
> *So pale, so stiff, so bare today,*
> *Never to play, never to play?*

Hadrian's successor was followed by the emperor Marcus Aurelius, who was, like Hadrian, a scholar, and who exemplifies a mood not yet seen before in Italy: the beginnings of spiritual weariness. Marcus Aurelius was physically frail and had a tendency to melancholy: a bas-relief portrait shows him with a sad, grave face. During his reign, tribes on the northern frontier were constantly launching attacks, and the Roman legions found it difficult to hold them back, partly because there was no longer the same patriotic martial instinct to be found among the citizens: men would cut off their thumbs to avoid military service. Appalled by the immensity of his task, Marcus Aurelius turned to Stoicism and there found the inner strength he needed to continue, under discouraging circumstances, the performance of his office.

Stoicism teaches that "virtue alone brings happiness"—virtue for its own sake, since there is no afterlife. In a little book of *Meditations* which he wrote for his own encouragement, Marcus Aurelius reasons with his soul from Stoic principles, urging it to flee vice and carnal pleasures. "Take care not to be Caesarified. . . . Keep yourself a simple and good man, uncorrupt, dignified, plain, a friend of justice. . . ." How far did Marcus Aurelius succeed? "By nature a good man," says the historian Dio Cassius, "his education and the moral training made him a far better one." Gossip tells of his wife's infidelities, yet he loved and honored her, and in his writings thanks her for a happy wedded life. Even less than Hadrian did Marcus Aurelius believe that the soul is immortal, so the mainspring of his good life was a plain sense of duty. His *Meditations* were practically unknown until their publication in 1558; one wonders what comment Saint Jerome and Saint Augustine would have made on a pagan who, except for his view of the soul, was almost a Christian.

It is significant that Hadrian's favorite city was Athens, not his native Rome, and that Marcus Aurelius, a born Roman, wrote his *Meditations* in Greek. Italy had begun to decline economically: the vineyards and olive groves of Spain and Gaul, as these lands profited from the *pax Romana,* stole the markets from the Italian producers in Italy itself, while the stabilization of frontiers had dried up the supply of slaves to work the increasingly large estates. This economic decline was accompanied by decay of the middle class. Few new men were rising to the top, with the result that the very rich became fossilized in old ways and habits of thought. Romans were still first-class lawyers—this was precisely because law depended on the past, on precedents—but from A.D. 100 Roman literature grew feeble. There was no fresh philosophic or scientific thinking, only erudition without critical judgment. Literary education consisted in the slavish imitation of inimitable models, such as Homer or Virgil, and no one dreamed of opening new vistas of thought. Only in Greece was the spirit of inquiry still to be found, and the leading writers of the second and third centuries, such as Pausanias and Diogenes Laërtius, wrote in Greek.

Intellectual unproductiveness was accompanied by growing technological backwardness. The Italians had become accustomed to conquering the Mediterranean world by force; as that force began to weaken, it should have been replaced by inventiveness, new products, and expanding trade. But in fact the Italians showed small talent as traders: everywhere the Syrians stole a march on them. Rome was a nonproductive city of state-fed idlers and high-echelon administrators, and Italy remained what it had always been, a rural land; on the other hand Greece, Asia Minor, and Egypt possessed large urban communities, where workshops turned out an increasing range of goods for sophisticated, demanding customers, and it was to the East that Italy's gold—much of it the fruit of Trajan's victories in Dacia—began to drain away. Romans were accustomed to reading portents in the flight of birds; this flight of gold was a more sinister omen, but they were powerless to read it.

Meanwhile, a change took place in the type of imperial rule. Marcus Aurelius died a philosopher's death in 180 and was succeeded by his son Lucius Aelius Aurelius Commodus. Commodus ends the period of civilian emperors (69–180) and inaugurates the period of emperors

who ruled through the power of the army (180–282). He was as unlike his father as was possible. Stupid, cowardly, physically strong, Commodus enjoyed life most when appearing as a gladiator (against unarmed opponents) or sparring in the wrestling ring. He had himself portrayed and worshiped as Hercules with club and lion's skin, dismissed his father's advisers, terrorized the senate by massacring some of its members, and ruled through a military elite, the Praetorian Guard. When he needed money, he resorted to confiscation and judicial murder. Government broke down, and Italy lay at the mercy of marauders.

Power turned Commodus' head and he caused himself to be represented as a god on the coinage. His end was brought about by a conspiracy at court. He had put away his wife, and lived with Marcia, a Christian woman. When she and several courtiers fell under his suspicion, they decided to forestall him, and one New Year's Eve caused a wrestler, with whom he regularly practiced, to strangle him.

Pertinax, who succeeded Commodus, was soon murdered by the Praetorian Guard. Then in 193 Lucius Septimius Severus became emperor. A North African, fierce and vindictive, he had had to fight for his throne; and on the strength of evidence contained in the correspondence of his fallen rival, he had twenty-nine senators condemned to death. Many important posts, formerly reserved for senators, he now gave to retired army officers, so that the whole tenor of government became military. Law cases were heard no longer in public but behind the closed doors of the imperial palace. But in the context of maintaining the empire, the worst act of Septimius Severus' reign was a decree permitting soldiers "to cohabit with women": that is, to reside with their wives or concubines in the camp town. This domesticated the legions and lessened their taste for mobile, adventurous warfare.

Septimius Severus was succeeded by his son Caracalla, who, at the beginning of his reign, had his brother and coruler murdered. Caracalla also persecuted the senate and increased the pay of the army. In Rome he built the Thermae of Caracalla, the largest and most magnificent baths of antiquity, but most of his life was spent fighting on the German frontier and in the Middle East. While marching against the Parthians he was murdered at the instigation of his prefect of the guard, who had fears for his own life.

The Villa Adriana, built by Hadrian as a personal retreat outside Rome, included an artificial island, a theater, baths, and a sumptuous palace.

Caracalla was succeeded by his fourteen-year-old relative Elagabalus, a depraved Syrian who identified himself with the Syrian sun god, caused himself to be adored in Rome, and initiated that worship of the sun which, within decades, was to become the official religion of the empire. He was murdered after only four years of rule.

Elagabalus' young cousin, Marcus Aurelius Alexander Severus, succeeded to the imperium. He too was a Syrian, but studious and well-meaning. In his private chapel he placed statues of the best of the deified emperors, as well as of Abraham, Christ, Orpheus, and the wonder-working neo-Pythagorean philosopher, Apollonius of Tyana. Unfortunately, he was a mother's boy in the weakest sense and lacked the will to implement the reforms of which he dreamed. When the Germans crossed the Rhine, and other tribes the Danube, Alexander Severus proved incapable of handling his armies, in which mutiny had become a common occurrence. In an uprising of troops at Mainz he and his mother were killed. Machiavelli was to cite this emperor as an example of how virtue without strength leads to catastrophe.

The leader of the rising against Alexander Severus was a soldier called Maximinus the Thracian. His parents were rude tribesmen from northern Europe: one an Alan, the other a Goth, and he had made his way up from the ranks largely by his huge physique—his wife's bracelet is said to have fitted his thumb. Such a man cared nothing for tradition, for Italy, or for the legal institutions of the empire. He was the first emperor who did not cause the senate to confirm his position, and the first emperor who never entered Rome during his reign.

Maximinus carried out successfully his immediate task of driving the Germans back both on the Rhine and the Danube. Then in Africa the peasants rebelled against heavy taxation and proclaimed the pro-consul, Gordian, and his son co-emperors. They were quickly defeated by troops loyal to Maximinus, but the same confusion of rival emperors was to recur often in future reigns, embroiling still further a system of government already weakened by repeated invasions. After a three-year reign Maximinus was killed by his own soldiers.

The pattern of mutiny and palace revolution continued. In the next forty-six years there were no less than sixteen emperors. It was a time of confusion, pretenders, cruelty, and general hardship. Invasion became more frequent. Under Valerian the empire was overrun by Per-

A first-century mosaic from Pompeii illustrates the variety of sea creatures to be found in the Mediterranean in ancient times.

sians and Germans, only to be won back again by Aurelian, one of many vigorous emperors to come from Illyricum (present-day Yugoslavia).

In 284 the troops proclaimed a new emperor with exceptional qualities of leadership and organization who, temporarily at least, was to shore up the battered system of government. His name was Diocletian, and like Aurelian, he came from Illyricum. He had raised himself by a military career, but he was primarily a statesman. Realizing that singlehanded he could not cope with all the barbarian invasions, he divided the rule into four: himself and a colleague as augusti of Eastern and Western empires, and two subordinate aides known as caesars. He himself chose to look after the East, which was increasingly the richest and most civilized part. This arrangement worked well, and throughout Diocletian's reign the tribes pressing on the frontiers were held off.

Diocletian was a tall, lean man with an iron will. He kept his colleagues on a tight rein. When one of them lost a battle through stupidity, Diocletian hurried up with reinforcements and compelled the unhappy man, clad in the purple, to run alongside his chariot for a full Roman mile without deigning to address him a single word. The colleague made no more stupid mistakes.

Diocletian saw the need for a superior central authority which could control not only the immense system of government but the far-flung legions, each tending to be loyal to its own general. Though not vain, he caused himself to be treated with the dignity of a god. He insisted on being called *dominus,* or lord, no longer allowed citizens free access to his presence, and introduced from Eastern ceremonial such practices as prostrations and kissing of the imperial foot. He swept away the hollow pretense of republicanism and frankly ruled as a monarch. The senate sank to the position of a municipal council for Rome under the supervision of the emperor's prefect. It can be said that with Diocletian the principate definitely came to an end, and rule by an uncontestedly monarchical emperor began.

Diocletian transformed the empire into a fortress prepared for a long siege and manned it with 400,000 troops. He increased the number of provinces by making each unit smaller, so that there were now altogether over a hundred, grouped into twelve "dioceses," each under a "vicar." Northern Italy became the diocese of Italia, southern Italy and the islands the diocese of Suburbicaria.

Commodus, son of Marcus Aurelius, is portrayed here as Hercules.
OVERLEAF: *A third-century Roman mosaic shows a chariot race.*

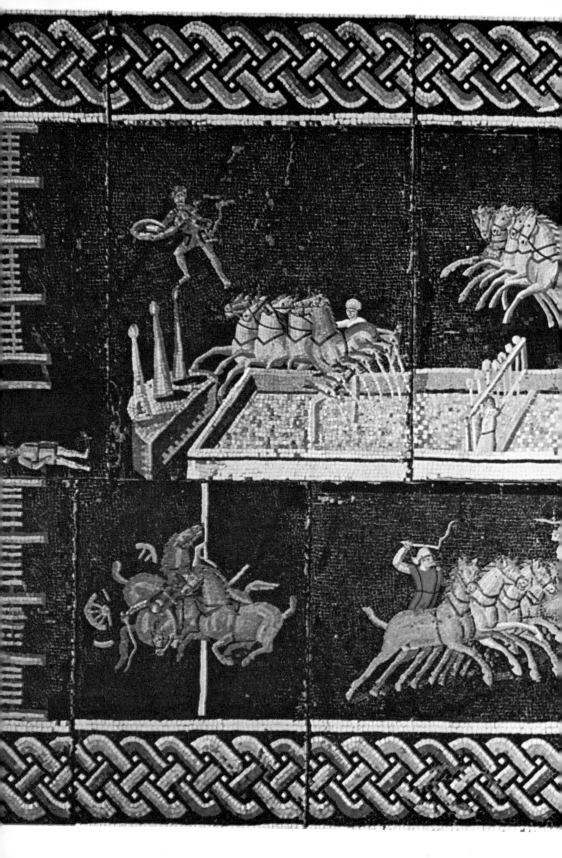

As a result of gigantic military expenditure, the empire had long suffered from inflation. In 301 Diocletian issued an edict of prices which typified the bureaucratic control now exercised over every aspect of life. The edict laid down a maximum price for every possible commodity of trade—about one thousand in all—and a maximum wage for every kind of service. Any trader who asked, or any purchaser who paid, a higher price was liable to death. No difference of locality or section was permitted. The edict was engraved on stone in every market in Roman Europe, but it did not end inflation.

By now Christianity had spread widely; Christians held high rank at court, in the army, and in the imperial hierarchy. For the first eighteen years of his reign Diocletian was well disposed toward them, and his wife was a Christian. In February, 303, however, for reasons that remain a mystery, but perhaps afraid that Christianity might become a cause of political faction, Diocletian issued an edict against the new sect. Churches were to be demolished or closed, their sacred vessels and scriptures surrendered. Degradation or slavery was decreed against them. Shortly afterward death was made the penalty for all who refused to renounce their faith. In Gaul and Britain the tolerant rule of Maximian, the Western augustus, kept martyrdoms to a handful, but in the East Diocletian ensured personally that thousands suffered torture and execution. What happened in Rome is uncertain. The Donatists, a heretical sect, spread a report that the bishop of Rome, Marcellinus, apostatized. This cannot be verified; what is certain is that communications between the Roman and Eastern Churches became cut for a time, with the result that the bishop of Rome's claims to supremacy were less heard and heeded in the East than in the West.

After a serious illness in 304 Diocletian no longer felt the energy indispensable for ruling a hundred million people, and the following spring he abdicated. He retired to his native Dalmatia and in Spoleto built a great palace which still stands. There he spent his remaining years quietly cultivating his garden. By regenerating this central power, he had added a hundred years of life to the waning empire.

As usual on the departure of an exceptional ruler a struggle followed for the succession. In 306 Maxentius, the son of Diocletian's co-ruler, seized Rome, where he was proclaimed augustus and ruled with cruelty, while in distant Britain Constantine was proclaimed emperor by

the Roman troops garrisoning York. In 312 Constantine gathered his
army—chiefly Germans, Celts, and Britons—led it over the Alps, won
a series of brilliant victories, and advanced on Rome, where Maxentius
had gathered a strong force. Constantine was a tough soldier who
when necessary did not hesitate to kill his kinsmen; like most men of
his day he also put great trust in omens, magic, and dreams. Shortly
before the battle with Maxentius, Constantine saw a vision of an angel
descending from Heaven with the sign of the cross and uttering the
words "In this sign you shall conquer." Still half pagan, Constantine
had a standard prepared bearing the letters X and P crossed to produce the contracted name of Christ, the Chi-Rho monogram.

When Constantine advanced on Rome Maxentius moved out from
the protecting walls and made his stand at Saxa Rubra, immediately
north of the city, with the Tiber at his back. Constantine was victorious,
and the beaten masses streamed back to the city over the only bridge,
the Milvian, which has given its name to the battle. The bridge
collapsed under the weight; Maxentius and part of his army were
drowned in the river, Constantine was greeted as a liberator, and the
senate erected in his honor a triumphal arch that still stands.

Constantine did not take a colleague as augustus; he ruled the empire alone. In Milan the following year, 313, he issued the famous
edict granting formal toleration to Christianity. The Christians were
by now quite numerous and winning new adherents, as a later emperor remarked, chiefly through their compassion for the poor and
their cult of the dead. Later Constantine was to become a Christian
himself, but he deferred his baptism to just before his death, in the
belief that baptism with its cleansing waters washes out all the sins
that have preceded it. He legislated in the spirit which Christianity
represented and which was supported by the religious and humanitarian ideas of the age, as when he abolished the old penalties for celi-
bacy, forbade frivolous divorce, and ended the gladiatorial games.

Christians clambered out of the catacombs and began to build the
first basilicas. Constantine himself is said to have begun the construction of the Lateran Basilica, Rome's future cathedral. In 321 Sunday
became an official holiday. But imperial gifts and favors involved imperial interference and patronage. In 314 the Donatists, dissatisfied
with a judgment by the bishop of Rome, Miltiades, appealed to Con-

stantine. The emperor received their appeal and referred the matter, though already judged by Miltiades, to a council of Western bishops assembled in Arles.

The geographical center of an empire stretching from Britain to Turkey was undoubtedly Rome, but from both an economic and military point of view Rome was losing importance and was no longer a satisfactory capital. It was the cities of the East that produced the most advanced goods and had the most prosperous trade, while the two military danger zones were along the Euphrates and the Middle Danube rivers. Diocletian had taken account of these facts when he chose to reside at Nicomedia near the Bosporus. Constantine went a step further: he decided to build a great new city at a strategically important town on the Bosporus called Byzantium, and to place this city,

Worship of the fertility goddess Diana was a popular devotion in the first century A.D. *In this fresco a procession of children bring offerings of wheat.*

which would bear his name, on a politically equal basis with Rome.

Constantine dedicated his city in 330. The court, the imperial government, the civil service, definitively moved 850 miles eastward, from old Rome to new Rome, as Constantinople was sometimes called. For two reasons the move is a turning point of history. First, it saved the Roman Empire, for the empire Constantine founded at Constantinople was destined to escape barbarian conquest and to endure for more than eleven hundred years. Second, it left old Rome to be thenceforward a center of spiritual authority under its bishop. Constantine and his successors saw themselves as head of the Christian Church. Had they remained in Rome they would have overshadowed the bishop; by their departure they left the bishop in Rome, like the bishops elsewhere, to shoulder more and more civil responsibilities, and eventually to play a leading part in resistance to the barbarians.

Under Constantine's successors the problem of barbarian invasion became increasingly acute. Across Eurasia millions were on the march. In 376 the Visigoths, a German people, petitioned the emperor Valens to be allowed to cross to the southern bank of the Danube, thus placing the broad waters of this river boundary between them and the fearsome, slant-eyed Huns, a Mongolian people, who were then sweeping out of the East. Probably 800,000 men, women, and children crossed the Danube and lived under the protection of Rome, while preserving their independence. The army was filled more and more with Germans, who retained the martial qualities Roman citizens had lost. It was an exception now for a Roman to rise to a top military post, and from this time onward purely German names begin to dominate the history of Europe.

Theodosius, who reigned from 379 to 395, was the last emperor to exert effective control over the whole empire. After his death, in 395, the two halves of the empire fell apart, one based in Rome, the other in Constantinople, and soon reached a state of mutual antagonism. In the West the emperor became a puppet in the hands of the master of the army, usually a German.

In Italy wealth began to dry up and taxation increased. As economic conditions deteriorated, the birth rate fell, and it has been estimated that the population of the empire at this period declined by as much as a third from its highest point. In the days of Scipio Africanus and

of Julius Caesar the legions had gained their battles over primitive tribes; now, however, those tribes had become organized nations, with a sense of purpose, and it is doubtful whether the legions at their best would have been able indefinitely to hold them back.

In Italy, as throughout the West, during the last centuries of the empire society grew more and more stereotyped. A man was compelled by law to follow the occupation of his father, were he a senator or a waterman on the Tiber, and he might not marry out of his guild or caste. Not even a dispensation from the imperial chancery, not even the growing power of the Church, could break this chain of servitude.

The land tax had become so heavy that many small proprietors had to sell up. In Campania alone, once the garden of Italy, more than 500,000 *jugera* (about 312,000 acres) went out of cultivation. In general, the middle class declined, while the very rich grew richer and so powerful that they were able with impunity to delay or evade payment of their taxes. They bribed the officers of the census to make false entries of property liable to taxation, and land inspectors to relieve them of the burden of unproductive estates. Some tax collectors were equally corrupt and repeatedly connived in the plutocrats' failure to pay their taxes.

The fine arts reflect these outward changes. From the fourth century, architects turn to designing walls and fortresses, sculptors leave their private clientele to concentrate on the emperor. As always in time of anxiety, the state tries to hide its weakness under bombast: typical is the colossal statue of Constantine, more like a Buddha than a Western work of art, of which the surviving head is now in the courtyard of the Palazzo dei Conservatori in Rome. A late Roman bronze statue of an emperor found in Barletta is no longer a portrait of a man but a hieroglyph of severity, designed to awe people into obedience.

When the senate erected an arch to Constantine, the creative urge to carve all the panels with scenes of victory was lacking, and several reliefs from the time of Trajan, Hadrian, and Marcus Aurelius were transferred from existing works. In the original carvings the moderation of the classical style has disappeared. The emperor, supernaturally large, towers over a uniform mass of marching soldiers, while the populace hanging on the emperor's words is represented by packed rows of ungainly bodies and plebeian heads; the molding of the bodies

The retarius *or "net-man" matched his skill with a weighted net and a trident against the more heavily armored sword-bearing gladiators in mortal sport.*

is imperfectly realized, the clothing is indicated in summary fashion by schematic lines, the movements are uniformly repetitive.

More and more sarcophagi are adorned with reliefs of battle, writhing masses of lunging soldiers and pain-racked wounded. Mosaic floors, as in the villa at Piazza Armerina in Sicily, depict hunting scenes in which the emphasis falls on carnage. Very common, especially in garrison towns, are statues of Mithras, the Persian god of light, plunging his dagger into the throat of a bull: Mithraism was for long a close rival of Christianity.

The growth of Christianity can be followed from the simple fresco paintings of the catacombs to the basilicas which in the fourth century became the typical form of Christian church. The roof of the basilica was of wood, and the width of the nave was limited by the length and strength of available beams so that two or more low side aisles were generally added. Whereas the Roman temple had been outwardly grand, the basilica was outwardly simple, with all its decoration—chiefly mosaic—concentrated within. Christians, who made a point of commemorating their dead, accorded special honor to martyrs, and many of the new churches were built above the tombs of Christians who had died for their faith. The most famous is the Basilica of Saint Peter which Constantine erected in 330 on the Vatican hill.

Christian sarcophagi depict Old and New Testament scenes in classical style, often more perfectly than secular work of the same period. The richest example is the sarcophagus of Junius Bassus, who according to his epitaph died aged forty-two as city prefect of Rome, in 359. Christ, here as was common elsewhere, is depicted as youthful and unbearded, though on one early tomb beneath the present Saint Peter's he appears with the horses and other attributes of the sun god. The crucifixion is never shown at this period, probably because it was such a demeaning form of death and early Christians wished to emphasize other aspects of their faith, such as charity, redemption, and the Second Coming.

Why did the Roman Empire decline and eventually fall? A partial answer is provided by Ammianus Marcellinus, the last of the great Roman historians, by birth a Greek, who wrote an account of the period 353 to 378. He attributes the decline to moral degeneration. Court society no longer honors the values upheld of old, officers are unfitted

Constantine's conversion, from his dream of the sign of the Cross to his victory over Maxentius, and his mother's discovery of the True Cross

for their posts, soldiers have become soft, officials are corrupt. However, he remains confident that Rome will emerge from her desperate plight, as from so many earlier reverses, and he exhorts the people to return to the simplicity and self-sacrifice of earlier generations.

Ammianus Marcellinus' answer is clearly unsatisfactory as it stands. Why the lowered moral standards? The answer is that society had become unbalanced and at the same time rigid, with a privileged upper crust still reaping personal advantage from political upheavals, while the urban bourgeoisie remained sunk in torpor and the masses were exploited. This imbalance was itself an effect of the main cause of decline: there just was not money enough for the frontier wars that went on and on and on. Even the richest modern nation would find it impossible to continue to fight on several fronts over a period of centuries. Throughout the Western provinces money became so scarce that it could not be come by honestly. Then moral standards declined. There finally came a point when there was no more money to equip the army adequately, and that point may be said to mark the fall of the Roman Empire.

At the moment when the edifice is ready to collapse, about the year 400, we may appropriately pause and consider the achievements of that empire. No country before or since has played a greater civilizing role than Italy in the almost five hundred years from Julius Caesar to the sack of Rome by Alaric. First in importance is the Latin language —concise, clear, and flexible—which came to be spoken in France, Spain, Portugal, and Rumania as well as, to a lesser extent, in Britain and North Africa. Until the sixteenth century, Latin was so prestigious a language that it remained the ordinary means of communication between educated Europeans, making possible a continuous dialogue even after the nation-states had evolved their own tongues. It is noteworthy that the impact of Latin was less pronounced in the German provinces, and from the fifth century German words began to leave their mark on the romance languages, especially in the sphere of warfare: *bellum* is replaced by *werra,* and German words are used for "shirt," "trousers," "pocket," "stirrup," and "spur."

Latin was the vehicle for the second great civilizing achievement: Roman law. The Roman had all the qualities of a lawyer—a sense of equity devoid of sentimentalism, an instinct for order, discipline,

A gallery of the Priscilla catacomb, part of the more-than-sixty-mile-long network of underground Christian burial places outside Rome

and business, and a devotion to ceremonies and formulae. The justice and precision of Roman law were such that Gallic and British communities hastened to learn Latin in order that they might gain the "Latin right," which admitted them to the privilege of enjoying Roman law. The Roman law always granted a right of appeal from a lower magistrate to his superior. This was the source of Paul's "appeal unto Caesar" from the procurator of Judaea, and this right is recognized today as one of the best means of protecting individual liberty.

In A.D. 212 Caracalla issued an edict whereby all freeborn provincial subjects became Roman citizens, thus concluding the protracted process of making Italy and the other regions of the empire equal before the law. Roman law was now accepted from the moors of Yorkshire to the rose-red desert town of Petra. It was under the Antonine emperors that some citizen from the East, only known to us by his praenomen of Gaius, wrote those learned *Institutes of Roman Law,* which are still studied by intending lawyers. Today the American and almost every European legal system are based upon Roman law, as is the canon law of the Catholic Church.

The third great legacy was an efficient system of government. In the late empire the emperor exercised his authority through high officials comparable to present-day ministers: for example, the Prefect of the Praetorium (Minister of the Interior), the Counts of the Treasuries (Ministers of Finance and Crown property), Quaestor of the Palace (Minister of Justice), and Masters of Troops (War Ministers). Executing the ministers' orders were civil servants, who constituted a new and elaborately graded nobility. Promotion was by seniority, and with the scale of functions went a scale of titles, some attached to the function itself and some conferred, as the crown of a man's career, when he retired. The civil service was in general humane, efficient, and impartial. Until the final years of decline and corruption, fiscal procurators collected the land tax with a minimum of harshness, and anyone who thought he had been overcharged could appeal to the emperor. In Judaea the Roman government was so tolerant of the religion of its Jewish subjects that even a Roman citizen who ventured to enter the Holy of Holies was punished with death.

One of the weaknesses of this governmental system was the absence of political liberty in the provinces. Provincial assemblies did meet:

they controlled local representatives of the government and reported flagrant abuses; but they never played, nor were they intended to play, a serious and constructive part in politics. Had they done so, new forces of vitality might have been released. It is unfortunate that the Roman Empire never knew representative government, any more than did the rest of antiquity.

Rome's last great civilizing achievements are her many building accomplishments: towns, roads, bridges, and aqueducts. Towns were planned in chessboard squares for communities dwelling under orderly government. Each was complete with its forum, temples, courts of justice, jails, baths, markets, and sewer system. The towns were linked by long, unswerving roads. Ordinarily, the road was made with a bottoming of large stones, often embedded in sand and covered with a surface of rammed gravel, the whole on an average eighteen inches thick. Milestones, sometimes inscribed with the distance from the nearest town, marked the whole length. Small stopping areas, where the officials of the imperial post carrying dispatches from Rome could secure fresh horses, were established every few miles; larger posting stations, with overnight accommodation provided, occurred at longer intervals.

Among the aqueducts the most famous are the so-called Pont du Gard in the south of France, built under Augustus to bring water to Nîmes, and the aqueduct of Segovia, in central Spain. The latter, built under Trajan, had 128 arches constructed of granite blocks without mortar or clamps, extending over a total length of 879 yards. The fact that both these giant engineering works have endured for almost two thousand years is visible proof of the extraordinary constructive achievement of the empire which had its source, its ideals, and its greatest men in Italy.

CHAPTER IV

THE DARK AGES

Τ he Roman Empire had been consolidated by the Latin language, Roman law, and the imperial bureaucracy, but ultimately what held it together were the legions. The money which paid the legions came largely from the tribute of the Eastern provinces. When in 330 Constantine moved the capital of the empire to Constantinople, less of that tribute reached the West, and Italy in particular. Moreover, fewer and fewer of the soldiers came from Italy; they were recruited now from the north. By the third century *barbarus* was the ordinary Latin word for soldier. If around 400 we look at Italy in the context of Europe, we are struck by her decline of energy. Not only are the legionaries drawn from outside Italy, but the philosophical schools are in Athens, the law schools in Beirut, the great library is in Alexandria, and manufactured goods come from the Eastern provinces.

In marked contrast to Italy's debility was the vigor of the Visigoths, who had recently crossed the Danube to live in part of Moesia (present-day Serbia and Bulgaria). In 395 Alaric was chosen leader of the Visigoths and set himself to find better, more extensive land within the Roman Empire on which his people could settle in security and

Built as a domed octagon in the Byzantine style, the Church of San Vitale, Ravenna, was consecrated by the Archbishop Maximian in 547.

peace, and where he himself would be recognized as an important Roman dignitary. First Alaric made a series of raids into Greece, but the Eastern emperor secured his withdrawal by appointing him *magister militum,* master of the soldiers, in Illyricum. Then Alaric decided to try his fortunes in Italy. In 401 he crossed the Alps. The Emperor of the West was 17-year-old Flavius Honorius. On the advice of Stilicho, his Vandal general, Honorius moved the imperial court from Rome to Ravenna, a city protected by marshes and capable of being reinforced from Constantinople. Stilicho drove Alaric out of Italy in 401, and again in 403. But the indefatigable Visigoths returned. This time the imperial troops failed to stop them, and in 410 Alaric entered Rome.

Not for eight hundred years had a foreign army forced its way into Rome. Though material damage to the city was slight, the psychological effect was enormous. It showed that Italians were no longer able even to defend their capital. Civilized but effete, they were no match for the tough men from the north. Though no one foresaw it at the time, this was only the first of many invasions from the north which for centuries were to lay Italy waste.

There was much speculation on the cause for Italy's collapse. Believers in the old gods claimed that by deserting Jupiter and Juno for Jesus Christ, Italians had incurred the anger of Heaven, and the fall of Rome was their punishment. Saint Augustine of Hippo replied in *The City of God* that even worse disasters happened in pre-Christian times, and that good Christians should know how to profit spiritually from temporal losses. Saint Augustine then went on to make the influential statements that the Church and State are separate and the State can only be part of the City of God by being submissive toward the Church in all religious matters.

In Italy the Visigoths found a far more civilized land than their own, and were prepared to learn from the people they had conquered. Alaric took as hostage Galla Placidia, half sister of Honorius, and when Alaric died, his successor, Ataulfus, took her as his wife. Ataulfus declared that he wanted to use the Gothic sword "not to overthrow the Empire but to restore and preserve it."

More invasions by other peoples followed. Attila the Hun burned towns in northern Italy but was persuaded by Pope Leo to spare Rome. Vandals from Carthage sacked Rome in 455, and again the court

moved to Ravenna. All the while the emperors were puppets of their
mainly barbarian generals. Finally, in 476 a general named Odoacer,
who had had a successful career as a soldier of fortune in the region
now known as Austria, struck out for himself. He pensioned off the
young emperor, Romulus Augustulus, with 6,000 gold pieces a year
and the former villa of the pleasure-loving Lucullus on the bay of
Naples; returned the regalia of emperor to Constantinople; and assumed the new title King of Italy, under the rule of Constantinople.

The enforced abdication of Romulus Augustulus was an important
political event, but not the end of a political system. Odoacer ruled
within the framework of the empire, and when he quarreled with his
nominal sovereign over Dalmatia, the emperor in Constantinople felt
free to call in yet another barbarian, Theodoric, to expel Odoacer.
Theodoric had spent ten years of boyhood as a hostage in Constantinople, and had there learned to admire Roman and Greek culture.
When he took the title King of Italy, although illiterate, he enforced
the law, cut taxes, repaired aqueducts, and encouraged agriculture. He
combined a northern energy, of which Italy stood sorely in need, with
respect for Italian civilization.

Although he paid lip service to Roman institutions, Theodoric really
governed through his Gothic military counts (the comitia) and his
privy council of Gothic nobles. He decreed that Italians might not bear
arms, except as mercenaries in the Gothic ranks; Italians were regarded by their conquerors merely as useful shopkeepers, tradesmen,
artists, and physicians. Theodoric built a palace at Ravenna which no
longer survives, and the basilica consecrated to Jesus Christ (Theodoric
was an Arian) and known since 800 as San Apollinare Nuovo. Its beautiful mosaics depict thirteen miracles of Christ and thirteen scenes from
his Passion, though not the Crucifixion, for Christian artists still shrank
from representing the dying Saviour.

One of Theodoric's most intelligent statesmen was a rich Roman
named Boethius. His wife was the daughter of one of the chief senators, and in 522 both his sons were made consuls, for the forms of the
ancient way of life persisted, even though the titles had been voided of
real power. Boethius was an expert on music, water clocks, astronomy;
he was also a patriot who believed that Rome would be better off without the Goths. One day Theodoric, instigated by his Gothic advisers,

accused Boethius of having in certain letters expressed hopes that Rome might recover her freedom. Boethius was thrown into prison in Pavia and his case referred to the senate. While in prison he composed a book entitled *The Consolation of Philosophy*. Philosophy appears to Boethius in the form of a lady; she reminds him of his former happiness—of his wife, his sons, his honors, his wealth. Boethius comments sadly: "In every adversity the worst kind of unhappiness is to have been happy." Philosophy points out that he still possesses the love of his family and much else that should make him happy, then inveighs against ambition and the desire for fame. Boethius begs her to explain to him the nature of true happiness. She replies that it consists in the contempt for all earthly things and in looking to God as the *summum bonum*. There is in the book no allusion to Christianity, but from earliest times Boethius was always regarded as a Christian, the tone of his book being so unworldly.

Boethius' book was the most widely read work of literature during what is conveniently termed the Dark Ages—it was translated by, among others, King Alfred and Chaucer—and in many ways it establishes the mood of Italy during that period. Man felt that he was no longer master of his fate; in a world of brute force and unpredictable tyrants the best thing was to lie low, avoid public life, and think of the world to come. That this was in fact the most prudent policy was underlined by Boethius' end. He seems to have been innocent, but the senate, doubtless overawed by Theodoric, found him guilty. A cord was tied round his head and tightened until his eyes almost bulged from their sockets; then his life was beaten out of him with clubs. A few months later his father-in-law, Symmachus, who openly expressed grief, was accused, loaded with chains, taken to Ravenna, and there put to death, probably with torture and certainly without any trial. Thus, in spite of his professed admiration for Roman law, Theodoric was, under his veneer of civilization, as cruel a tyrant as the worst of the Roman emperors.

One Italian who felt like Boethius was Benedict, of Nursia, a little town in the Umbrian Apennines. In 495 the fifteen-year-old Benedict went to study in Rome—then under the rule of Odoacer—but he quickly became disgusted with the immorality of his fellow students and withdrew to a cave near Subiaco, in the mountains about forty-five miles from Rome. There he spent three years as a hermit. He won a reputation for holiness and was chosen as abbot by the monks of nearby Vicovaro. When Benedict began a series of reforms, the monks regretted their choice and tried to poison him, whereupon Benedict returned to his cave. But he was joined by many others who believed that it was impossible to lead a Christian life in society as it then was; some of his followers belonged to the best families of Rome. Benedict divided them into small communities, living off the land.

Monasticism until Benedict's time had retained the marks of its Egyptian origin: it was characterized by contemplation and extreme asceticism, which deterred men of gentle birth from becoming monks. Benedict realized that something less severe was needed, and he wrote a Rule for his monks which can be summarized in the phrase *Ora et Labora,* Pray and Work. Prayer had always been a staple of monastic life, but the idea of monks doing manual work as a way of praising God and of taming their passions was an innovation, and one that was to prove enormously successful. Each monastery under the Benedictine rule became a self-contained unit producing its own corn, oil, and wine. All that was best in the old Roman political system was embodied in the Rule, the key words of which are authority, gravity, stability, and moderation. All distinctions of class or race were set aside, and leisure was forbidden as an enemy of the soul.

In 529 Benedict founded a monastery at Monte Cassino, which throughout the Dark Ages was to shelter manuscript Bibles, sacred commentaries, and the classics, as well as to uphold Christian ideals. Toward the end of his life Benedict was joined by his sister, Scholastica, who took up her residence in a cell some distance from the monastery. Benedict died in March, 543, and his body, with that of his sister,

A gold fibula worn by one of the Lombard barbarians who swept down from the north to conquer Italy in the sixth century

CARCER.IN PAPIA. CI VITATE. PHILOSOPHIA.

Boetius Senator.

Flebilis heu m estos cogor inire...

lies in the abbey church of Monte Cassino. For seven centuries, until the days of Saint Francis and Saint Dominic, the Benedictines were the only Order of Western Christianity, and at one time they had no fewer than forty thousand monasteries and priories.

If the old Republican virtues were codified and perfected in an ecclesiastical context by Saint Benedict, the old Roman law was codified in a secular context by the emperor Justinian. This important codification was to be described by Dante as "mending the bridle of Italy." During the years 530–535 Justinian's commissioners drew up the Codex of imperial edicts, decrees, and so forth, in twelve books; the Pandects in fifty books, which is a compendium of some 2,000 volumes of the old laws and *senatus consulta* of Rome; and a shorter manual in four books called the Institutes. Their authors wrote in silver-age Latin, and by removing what was useless and redundant, preserved for future generations the old notion of equity which had been evolved in the early days of Rome.

Justinian is in many ways the greatest of the Eastern emperors. Although he reigned in Constantinople, he had never forgotten that the empire had formerly been undivided, and in 535 he decided that he was strong enough to attempt the reconquest of Italy. He had a good general, an Illyrian named Belisarius, who had already reconquered North Africa. Belisarius won Sicily, then swept up from the south and captured Rome. He was then replaced by Narses—an unlikely general, since he was an Armenian eunuch aged seventy-five—and in 553 Narses eventually drove the last of the Goths beyond the Alps.

Italy was once again part of the empire, and although the reunion lasted less than twenty years, it is symbolized by a pair of beautiful Byzantine churches erected under the patronage of Justinian in Ravenna: San Apollinare in Classe and San Vitale. The latter contains mosaics portraying Justinian and his wife Theodora, a former circus dancer. Although we know that she was rather short, Theodora, in her jeweled crown, is portrayed as the tallest figure in a group of ten priests and handmaidens. Certainly she had an ascendancy over the Byzantine court, and Justinian attributed the wisdom of many of his laws "to the sage counsel of his most revered consort."

The golden and purple mosaics of Ravenna are like a sunset before the dark night which fell on Italy with the invasion of the Lombards

Boethius wrote his famous Consolation of Philosophy *while in prison.*
OVERLEAF: *The emperor's submission to papal authority is symbolized here.*

in 568. According to Paul the Deacon, a historian who died about 800 and himself a Lombard, the Lombards were a Germanic people originating, like the Visigoths, in Scandinavia. During the reign of Augustus they were dwelling along the banks of the Lower Elbe, and by about 500 they had established themselves on the northern banks of the Danube. Their ferocity was a byword and their king, Alboin, having slain another barbarian king, married his daughter, and forced her to drink from a cup made of her father's skull.

In the second half of the sixth century the Lombards swept over the Alps and occupied an area which included modern Lombardy and the greater part of Venezia, Liguria, and Tuscany. Independent Lombard warriors penetrated farther south and founded the duchies of Spoleto and Beneventum. The king of the Lombards had his capital in Pavia, and divided his conquests among thirty-six dukes. Who now was to save the Italians? The center and extreme south of Italy still belonged theoretically to the Byzantine emperor, but his hold was getting weaker. Increasingly, in their struggle against the Lombards, the people of Italy looked not to Ravenna but to Rome, where the bishop was emerging as a leading poltical figure.

At a very early period in the history of Christianity, the bishops of Rome were faced with an epoch-making choice. Pious Christians bequeathed goods and land to the Church, and the bishops had to decide whether to decline or accept these legacies. If they accepted, they would of course eventually grow rich and powerful. They did in fact accept, becoming first owners of large estates, then by the sixth century rulers of extensive territories, dukes of Rome in all but name. The popes had no liking for the Lombards, but saw the necessity of playing off the Byzantine emperor's representative, known as the exarch, against the Lombard king.

The Lombards by degrees became fairly civilized, as two examples show: in 749 King Ratchis abdicated in order to end his days at Monte Cassino, and King Desiderius patronized scholars, while his daughter, we are told, learned by heart "the golden maxims of philosophy and the gems of poetry." But the kings saw no reason why they should not rule all Italy; they constantly made life difficult for the popes.

Pope Paul I was on his deathbed but still alive when the duke of Nepi (a little town of the papal-Roman duchy) hastened to Rome and

set his brother Constantine on the papal throne. As Constantine was a
layman, he had to be ordained cleric, subdeacon, deacon, and priest, and then consecrated as bishop and pope, all on the same day. A year later a priest, Philip by name, was put forward by the Lombard faction. He was consecrated in the Lateran and gave his papal benediction to the congregation in Saint Peter's. But the next month a third pope, Stephen III, was elected by a combination of clerics, army, and the people. "This new election," according to the historian Pasquale Villari, "did not allay popular excitement, since before the new pope was consecrated the victorious party decided to take vengeance on Constantine and his adherents. Some of these had eyes and tongue torn out. The infuriated mob then rushed to the house in which Constantine was confined. They overwhelmed him with insults, set him on horseback on a woman's saddle, and took him to a monastery. Thence he was conducted to the Lateran, where the assembled bishops deposed him, stripping off his pallium and his pontifical leggings. Shortly after this his enemies dragged him out of the monastery, dug out his eyes, and left him lying on the street almost dead."

That unedifying drama was typical of a situation where the Lombards encroached on papal prerogatives. The papacy naturally wished to end such scandals and believed that the best means of doing so was to increase its power and the extent of its territory. Just about this time, the emperor in Constantinople lost his last hold on Italy, when Ravenna fell to the Lombards and the exarchate ceased to exist. The pope wished to claim as his the Italian lands which had comprised the exarchate, and in the second half of the eighth century the document known as the Donation of Constantine was forged by a papal notary. It purported to be a grant made by Constantine, on the removal of his capital to the East, to Pope Sylvester, handing over to him "the city of Rome and all the provinces and cities of Italy" to be governed by him and his successors in perpetuity. This document sanctioned papal rule in the former exarchate as well as in Rome and its environs.

Now that the popes could no longer look to Constantinople for help, they sought some other ally who would prevent the Lombards from absorbing Rome into their state and would also perhaps implement the terms of the Donation of Constantine. In 755 Pope Stephen II called in Pepin, the newly elected king of the Franks, to subdue Aistulf, the

OVERLEAF: *Manuscript preserving was an important task of medieval monks. Here Saint Jerome dictates his version of the Bible to scribes.*

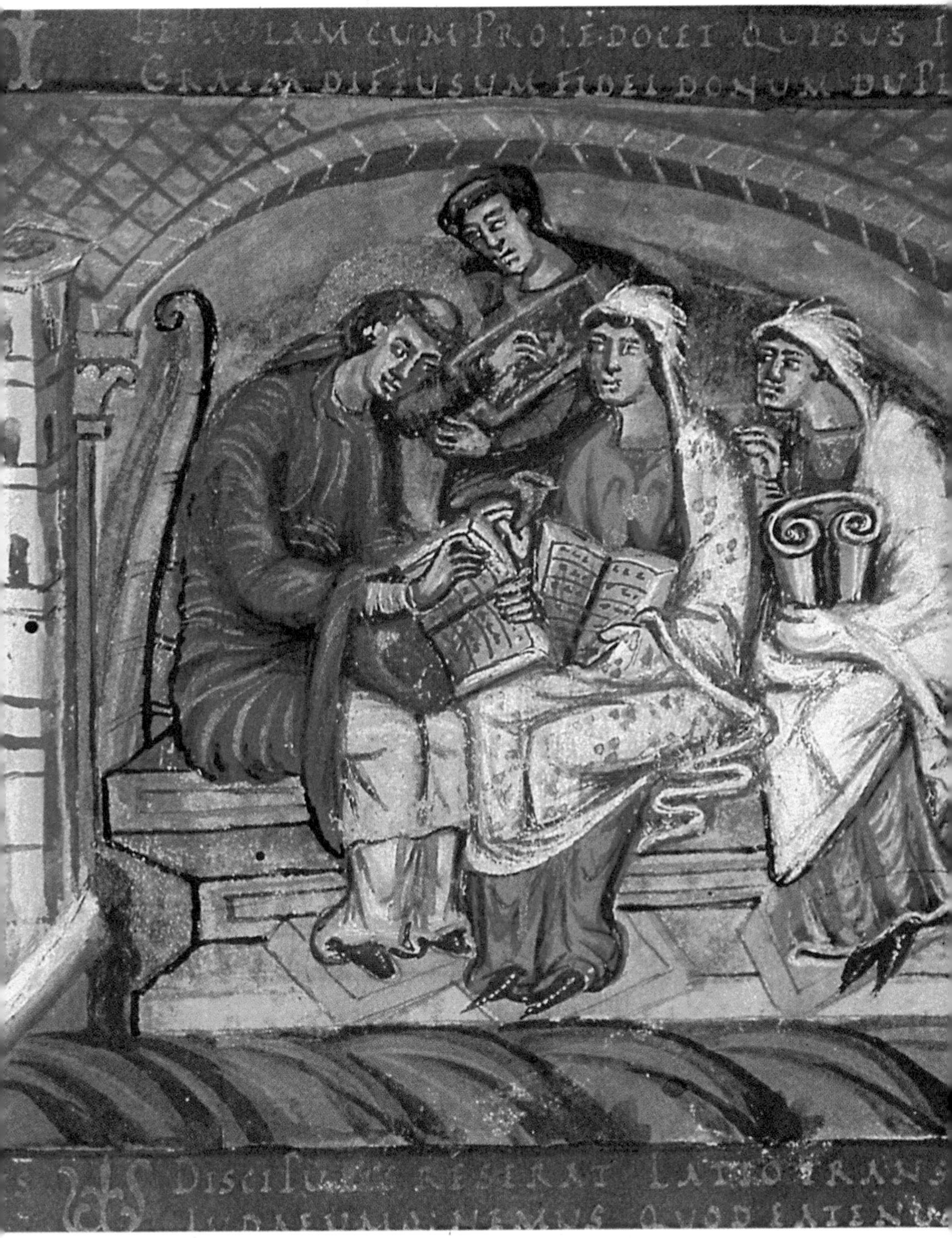

Lombard king. This Pepin did, forcing Aistulf to yield Ravenna and more than twenty other towns. These were still legally the property of the Eastern emperor, but the pope, invoking the forged Donation, accepted them from Pepin as his. The papacy thereby assumed control of a wide belt of territory slanting across the central peninsula, which, until 1870, was to comprise the Papal States.

The Lombards continued to make trouble, and once more the popes turned for help to the Franks. Pepin's successor, Charlemagne, crossed the Alps, subdued the Lombards, and himself took the title King of the Lombards. On Christmas Day, 800, in Saint Peter's, the pope crowned Charlemagne Emperor of the West. Charlemagne did not ask for this new title, nor did he use it for some time, but eventually he resigned himself to it. The title Emperor implied that the man who bore it was the leader of the lay section of Christendom. In future it was taken for granted that it was the emperor's job to intervene at Rome when scandalous elections occurred.

It was a new idea that the pope should crown an emperor, and in the sense that this implied that temporal rulers were subject to spiritual authority, the coronation ushered in a new era for Italy. In what may be termed the second half of the Dark Ages, society changed, in theory at least, from a secular to a clerical structure.

At the same time a new external force began to make itself felt, namely Islam. The Moslems had invaded the formerly Roman territories of North Africa; they had conquered Spain and invaded southern France, being halted at Poitiers by Charlemagne's grandfather, Charles Martel. Their impact on Italy was not so dramatic, but none the less damaging. In 827 they invaded Sicily with 100 ships and 11,000 soldiers, captured the island—where they were to remain for two centuries—and from there harried the coast of southern Italy. In 846 they sailed up the Tiber and sacked the country as far as the walls of Rome. But three years later their fleet was sunk by a Neapolitan squadron. In 883 they destroyed the great Benedictine abbey of Monte Cassino. Far into the tenth century Italy was to suffer not only from traditional northern invaders but from these Saracens based in Sicily.

The two centuries between 830 and 1030 mark the lowest ebb of civilization in Italy. Apart from chronicler monks the only writer worth mentioning is Liudprant, bishop of Cremona, who produced a

history of the period 887–962. With the breakup of the Carolingian
Empire, no emperor was strong enough to ensure fair papal elections, and within eight years (896–904) there were no less than ten popes, most of whom gained or lost their office by criminal intrigue or murder.

But as the Carolingian Empire collapsed, a powerful new ruler arose in Saxony, by name Otto the Great. He wished to establish his authority in Germany and in order to gain the title Emperor of the West was prepared to play an active part in Italy. In 962 Otto was crowned emperor by the pope, and the occasion was taken to regulate the relations between the new German Empire and the Holy See. Otto promised to restore the Carolingian Donation, which the Church had allowed to let slip from its grasp, thus making the pope the lord of a large part of central Italy, and of considerable domains in other parts of Italy. The emperor was to have permanent representatives in Rome. No papal election could be made without their participation. They were not to have a voice in choosing the pope, but the pope-elect must swear an oath of fealty to the emperor and obtain recognition in return before he could be consecrated.

The revival of imperial power by Otto and his line brought to Italy increased security, the renewal of commerce, and the expansion of civic life. Much of Italy and Germany were now united under a single ruler, and during the coming centuries the king elected by the German nobles became, as of right, king of Italy, and a candidate for coronation as emperor. On the other hand, papal lawyers argued that since the business of human life was to save souls, civil society had to be organized in subordination to that end: and this meant the subordination of emperor and kings to the Church. The ceremony of coronation which the Church had invented, largely drawn from the Old Testament and the anointing of Saul by the prophet Samuel, was intended to give emperor and kings a high sense of their Christian responsibilities. They assumed duties which gave them the right to the obedience of their subjects. But if they failed to fulfill these duties, they could forfeit their position, and of this the pope was to be the judge. It was the opening of a struggle between Church and State that was to last for centuries. It became very easy for the popes to decide that any ruler who opposed them was thereby unfit to rule over Christians, and threats of excommunication were to become part of papal policy.

CHAPTER V

RISE OF
THE CITY-STATES

D̲uring the ten centuries between 400 and 1402, when a German emperor was to make his last, unsuccessful attempt to intervene in Italian affairs, Italy was subject to foreign domination, but no foreigner succeeded in imposing his rule on the whole peninsula. In part this was due to geography: Italy, divided down the center by the Apennines, and with its long coastline, is particularly difficult to conquer or to unify. But there were two other factors. First, the memory of the Roman Republic, when Italy had been a great independent nation, was never extinct, and prompted at least in some a patriotic resistance to foreign domination. Second was the strong municipal feeling. During centuries of war, which isolated the regions, each city and town, with its surrounding countryside, came to rely on its own efforts and to forge communal institutions. It may be that vestiges of the old Roman system of municipal self-government lingered on, coalescing loyalties round this small unit.

At some crisis in the life of a city or large town the citizens would enter into a mutual understanding for concerted action and, to carry it out, would elect officials called consuls. The election of consuls was

The construction of the white marble cathedral of Pisa was begun in 1063 by a citizenry grateful for victory over the Saracens.

the first sign that a commune had been founded. They are mentioned in Pisa in 1084, in Milan thirteen years later. The next step was to obtain civic rights and privileges by charter, and this impecunious emperors were often ready to cede in exchange for military aid.

The communal movement began in the maritime cities. Because of their geographical position they were best able to elude control by either emperor or pope, and because of the wealth their citizens acquired by trade, there came to the fore a new class of wealthy merchants. Pisa is the earliest example. The Pisans built up a strong fleet, conquered Sardinia and Corsica, and in 1114 captured the Balearic Islands. In 1135 they smashed their nearest business rival, Amalfi. Pisan wealth was immense: proof of it survives today in the three remarkable white marble buildings constructed between 1063 and 1278: the cathedral, the baptistery, and the campanile or Leaning Tower. The wealthy merchants appointed consuls, varying in number from one city to the next, to represent their interests. These consuls at first ranked immediately after the bishop and the chief judge, but by the twelfth century had become the most important men in the city. Pisa recognized the temporal authority of the emperor and the spiritual authority of the pope, but insisted that both rulers respect her communal interests.

Municipal patriotism was purely local, and as soon as a city attained power she rounded on her rivals. Having crushed Amalfi, Pisa challenged Genoa, by whom she was eventually crushed. Genoa, from 1270, was ruled by a popular party, and was mistress of the seas from 1284 until her defeat in 1380 by Venice.

Among the rich mercantile cities Venice holds a special position. Impregnable amid her lagoons, Venice was an oligarchy, ruled by a "great council," whose members were all of aristocratic birth. She handled the extremely profitable trade between the East and northern Europe; she benefited also from the carriage of pilgrims to the Holy Land, and of the army during the Fourth Crusade.

Of the inland cities the most populous was Milan. Being so close to the Brenner Pass, Milan was particularly vulnerable to the many tides of northern invaders, and although republican consuls are first heard of around 1100 the city could not survive without the unity imparted by a single family. In 1277 the Visconti seized power, and were to hold it until 1447, a comparatively long time for an Italian medieval dynasty. Nearby Verona also accepted the benevolent despotism of a single family, the della Scalas (Scaligers). Eight successive della Scalas governed the city from 1262 to 1387.

The growth of the communal spirit should not be equated with a democratic movement. Often despots were in control, and it was only in the second half of the thirteenth century, and then only in some cities, that what may be termed a democratic movement gathered force with the winning of political power by members of the guilds. The prime example is Florence.

Florence stands well down the peninsula in the lee of the Apennines, and was therefore better placed than Milan or Verona to work out her own destiny. On the other hand she lacked the favorable trading position of Venice or her near neighbor Pisa. To compensate for this the Florentines had to work hard. They imported wool from as far afield as Portugal and the Cotswolds of England and turned this into some of the world's best cloth. They also developed an international reputation as bankers, eventually becoming bankers to the pope. By the thirteenth century they had made their gold florin, stamped with the effigy of their patron, John the Baptist, Europe's most wanted currency.

In the second half of the twelfth century the feudal nobility were still strong in Florence, and the city was dominated by seventy-five tall towers belonging to noblemen's houses, from which this or that nobleman's soldiers could shoot down troublemakers in the streets below. But the merchants and bankers were able to enrich themselves from trade faster than the noblemen from their estates or the booty of occasional wars. A long struggle culminated in 1267 with victory for the new business class. Rule now passed to the major guilds—wool manufacturers and merchants, judges and notaries, money changers, silk merchants, doctors and apothecaries—who elected for a two-month term of office executives similar to consuls called priors. The Florentines built a new seat of government, the Palazzo della Signoria, now known as the Palazzo Vecchio, the cornerstone of which was laid in 1298. It is a strongly fortified building, for Florence, like most Italian cities, was constantly troubled by party faction and wars with neighbors.

Southern Italy, with rare exceptions, did not share in this rise of the city-states. Its history followed a different pattern as a result of the Norman invasion. At the time when William the Conqueror was lead-

OVERLEAF: *The daily labors of the Tuscan peasants are depicted in this four-teenth-century fresco from the Palazzo Pubblico, Siena.*

ing his successful invasion of Britain, other Norman knights, led by the brothers William and Drogo of Hauteville, rode into Italy in search of wealth and land. Their numbers were small but they were excellent horsemen and used the stirrup, which was seemingly unknown to Italians. The Normans conquered southern Italy and Sicily and established their court in Palermo, where they adopted many of the customs of the Saracens they ousted. The Norman kings of Sicily, of whom the greatest is Roger II, ruler for fifty-three years, from 1101 to 1154, became patrons, like their Arab predecessors, of poets, philosophers, and artists. They allowed their Moslem subjects religious liberty—a remarkable concession in a period known for intolerance—but they also protected and enriched the Church. Among the witnesses to the century of Norman rule in Sicily are the Cappella Palatina, or royal chapel, in Palermo and the cathedral in nearby Monreale. Both are adorned with extensive and magnificent mosaics, the finest in Italy after those of Ravenna. But of course the Normans ruled as absolute kings, and brought in feudalism; as a result there was in southern Italy no communal development either now or under the Normans' successors, first the Angevins, then the Aragonese, comparable to that in the north.

Rome too failed to share in this rise of the city-states. True, the republican spirit never wholly died in Rome—it flared up for a moment in the person of Cola di Rienzi, who headed an unsuccessful popular rising and was killed in 1354. But Rome was not a manufacturing or commercial city—what little wealth it had came either from pilgrims or from providing for the papal curia—and so a strong middle class failed to develop. Even if it had developed, the pope was now so powerful a figure as to be unchallengeable by any group of citizens.

The pope, however, could be, and frequently was, challenged by the emperor. For exactly a century, from 1076 to 1176, these two powers were locked in a struggle as to which one should invest bishops within the Holy Roman Empire. The question was important, because the Church had now become so rich that about half the territory of the empire belonged to bishops. If the pope were to appoint new bishops, without the consent of the emperor, then the pope would become monarch of half the empire. On the other hand, the pope could not allow the emperor alone to make such appointments, for then the Church would be subject to temporal rule. In essence, the investiture

The emblem of Milan's powerful Visconti family was a man-eating serpent, displayed here on a helmet and shield held by a mysterious lady.

question was a new manifestation of the old fundamental problem with which the Church had burdened herself when she agreed to accept large bequests of land.

During the investiture struggle both pope and emperor sought allies among the new city-states. The pope's supporters were known as Guelphs, the emperor's as Ghibellines; but often the labels were used to disguise communal ambitions. The investiture dispute was settled by a compromise in 1122, the emperor retaining a large measure of control over episcopal elections, especially in Germany, the pope receiving forever the right of investiture with ring and staff. The dispute had weakened the authority of the emperor in Italy, and some vassals took occasion to throw off the yoke of their suzerain.

The struggle between emperor and pope continued even after this settlement of the investiture question. In 1154, Emperor Frederick I (Barbarossa) swooped down upon certain cities of Lombardy and crushed their budding independence. When Frederick departed, the cities, burying local differences, banded together in a "Lombard League," with the pope's encouragement. In 1176 at Legnano, eleven miles from Milan, the forces of the League won a crushing victory over Frederick's German knights. This gave a great impetus to republicanism and local autonomy. The next year a settlement was made in Venice. Barbarossa humbly kissed the pope's foot and agreed that the cities of the Lombard League might govern themselves according to their republican principles, giving him only a nominal overlordship. This was the first time republican envoys had ever met a pope or an emperor on equal terms: a sign that the city-state had come of age.

The wealth and power of bishops which had given rise to the investiture dispute produced, by reaction, a quite different and more fruitful movement in the person of Francis Bernardone of Assisi. Francis' father was a rich draper who traveled much on business, particularly in France, a country he liked and after which he named his son. Young Francis learned French, including the troubadour poems with their praise of chivalry. He took part in political street clashes and in one of the innumerable wars of the period was captured by the Perugians. While in prison in Perugia his soul was touched by grace. He came to see the futility of wealth and the wars to which wealth gave rise, and on his release he decided to lead a life of complete poverty. Poverty

A detail from "Massacre of the Innocents," by the Sienese painter Duccio

EL MEZO DE
L CHAN INO
D NOSTRA
VITA MIRI
T ROVA IN
P UNA SEL
VA SCURA
CHE LA DRI
T A VI A ER
A SMARIT

A QUANTA
P IR QUALE
IE COSA D
V RA QVE
S TA SILVA
S ILVAGGI
A S PR A E T
FORTE CH
E NEL PEN
S IER RINO

and humility had for a long time been preached in Italy, often as a form of protest against corrupt ecclesiastical authorities and their political patrons and partisans. Francis, however, brought to the movement a new gentleness which was to win all hearts.

In 1206, at the age of twenty-four, Francis renounced all his possessions, and wearing a rough woollen garment girt with a rope, went off to preach poverty and humility. He had, he said using the terminology of troubadour poems, "married my lady Poverty," and in all his preachings and writings there is a note of joy, as of one newly married: joy not only in God, but in the God-given beauty of Nature. "Let the brothers take care not to appear sad or gloomy," wrote Francis. God's troubadour, the peasants called him, for "drunken with the love and pity of Christ," Francis would often take two sticks and pretend he was "drawing a bow across a violin and with fitting gestures would sing in French of the Lord Jesus Christ."

Out of humility Francis never became a priest. In 1210, with eleven companions, he went to the pope to ask approval for what was to become the Franciscan Order. Later he sent missions into France, and he himself traveled to Egypt in an unsuccessful attempt to convert the sultan. But most of his life was spent in the simple task of preaching in his native Umbria, interspersed with periods of retirement to Mount Verna, during one of which he received the stigmata. He died in 1226, and the fact that he was canonized only two years later shows how widely and deeply he had left his mark in a short lifetime.

By stressing the brotherhood of men, the Franciscan spirit cut across the old differences of race and civic rivalry. The relationship preached by Francis was that of brother to brother, not father to son or master to slave, and in this sense it was to prove influential in the development of individual rights within the new city-states. Although the Order was soon sharply divided between the Zealots, who clung to a strict interpretation of the vow of poverty, and the Moderates, who would allow the Order to possess property, the Franciscans flourished, expanded, and became one of the most important influences for good in Italian life. Even today the Franciscan friary, with its cloistered garden for meditation, and its brown-robed, sandaled friars tending the poor and sick, is a familiar sight in almost every Italian town.

After Francis' death, a memorial church was built in Assisi and

This 1465 portrait of Dante Alighieri by Domenico di Michelino is thought to be one of the earliest individualized portraits of the poet.

decorated by Giotto. It is no accident that Giotto and his followers took a new interest in the world about them, and in the beauties of Nature saw a reflection of God, for Francis had opened their eyes by his canticles in praise of the sun, the moon, the birds, animals, and flowers. The Franciscans in their sermons also brought a more homely, emotional approach to the truths of Christianity; they fastened on picturesque details in the early life of Christ, and these too provided new subjects or telling touches for the painters.

The other great saint of thirteenth-century Italy could hardly be more different from Francis. Thomas Aquinas was born in the castle of Roccasecca about 1225. His father was related to the emperors, his mother to the Norman kings. He studied at Monte Cassino and at the university of Naples, then joined the other great Order of friars which had come into being within a few years of Saint Francis' fraternity: the Dominicans. His family disapproved and brought Thomas home. But the emperor Frederick II stepped in and ordered the young postulant's release. Thomas then went to Cologne, where he studied under Albert the Great. Albert had himself been a student at Padua, where some of the works of Aristotle circulated in translations from the Arabic made at the court of the Sicilian kings. Thomas Aquinas recognized the importance of Aristotle's philosophic system—the greatest evolved in antiquity—and the part it could play in providing a reasoned explanation of the universe compatible with Christianity. He decided to devote his life to writing a system of philosophy which would, so to speak, baptize the great Greek. In the *Summa theologica* Aquinas built a complete structure of Christian theology based on human reason enlightened by divine revelation. He taught that faith and science, theology and philosophy, could not contradict, since God was the source of all truth. He succeeded in persuading the Church that Aristotle's system was to be preferred to Plato's as the basis of Christian philosophy, thus leaving a permanent mark on the educational system of the Christian West.

Thomas Aquinas taught for a time at the university of Bologna, which had the best law faculty in Europe, and since Bologna lay in the Papal States, many of the papal canon lawyers took their degrees there. The university of Padua specialized in natural science, the university of Salerno in medicine, particularly the herbal medicine practiced by

Medieval defensive towers still dominate the townscape of San Gimignano, once an important center of Tuscany.

the Arabs. Frederick II, who himself knew six languages and had an interest in medicine, had founded the university at Naples in 1224. These new centers of learning would have been unthinkable before the eleventh and twelfth centuries; they show that war was at last letting up and that some Italians at least now possessed the money, the time, and the spirit of independence required to pursue studies which, outside the courts, had been neglected since the first inroad of barbarians seven hundred years before.

Whereas Thomas Aquinas tried to systematize all knowledge in a single great theological treatise, Dante tried to systematize Italian life, present and past, in a single great epic poem. Dante Alighieri was born in Florence in 1265 of well-considered but not rich parents. He played an active part in politics, serving his city as ambassador. In 1302, as one of the six priors, he rejected a demand from the pope that would have curtailed Florence's independence. The city was divided on the issue, blood flowed, and Dante was sent, with one or two others, to attempt a reconciliation. During his absence the pope induced Florence to accept a "mediator," a royal and far from impartial adventurer named Charles of Valois. No sooner were the gates opened to him and his troops than Charles turned over the city to the feudal party opposed to Dante. They confiscated the poet's property and condemned him to death should he ever be caught in Florentine territory. Leaving his wife and four children behind, Dante was obliged to spend the rest of his life a wandering exile in the northern half of Italy.

The Comedy of Dante Alighieri, a Florentine by birth but not in character was the title given by the author to his work. "Comedy" meant the narrative of a happy escape from misery; the epithet "divine" was attached to it only centuries later by an admiring public. The poem takes the form of a journey through Hell and Purgatory to Heaven, and in this sense is an escape from misery. At each stage Dante meets historical figures who are expiating evil deeds on earth or enjoying the rewards of virtue. With the detachment made possible by exile, Dante sets every aspect of Italian society within the framework of eternity. In the center of Hell he places Judas, with Brutus and Cassius, who also betrayed their master and benefactor, Caesar. Among those he meets in Paradise are the emperor Justinian and Saint Benedict.

As a political thinker Dante saw that intercity strife was ruining

Saint Francis preaches a sermon to the birds in a famous painting by Giotto.

Italy. Dante pinned his hopes on Henry VII, the new emperor who proposed to make peace between Church and Empire. But the idealistic young reformer failed in his Italian enterprise and died in 1313. Eight years later Dante himself died, still an exile, deeply disappointed at his hero's failure.

Dante's hope of an Italy united by a strong man from beyond the Alps was already badly outdated during the poet's lifetime and destined never to happen. Instead, Dante himself gave Italy a quite different but no less vital unity: that of language. Since the time of the invasions Latin had steadily been barbarized; and when Otto was crowned, the people of northern Italy spoke a *lingua volgare,* beginning to have an Italian sound, while in the south, Greek was spoken. In Dante's day each city had its own Italian dialect, while educated men wrote their letters and books in Latin. By choosing to write his *Comedy* in his native Florentine, Dante struck a blow for the vernacular against Latin. So many Italians memorized parts of the *Comedy* that Italian in its Florentine form became a new *lingua franca,* soon to replace Latin as the ordinary medium of communication among all classes of men. Even more than Shakespeare to the English or Corneille to the French, Dante remains to this day a living influence on Italians.

As the power of the German emperors declined, it might have been thought that Italy at last was to enjoy a respite from foreign influence and its accompanying rivalries and wars. But this was not to be. France had now become a great nation-state, and in order to exert a certain control over the Church, in 1309 King Philip the Fair moved the papacy to Avignon. This was to remain the papal seat until 1378. During that period the popes were Frenchmen. Many were holy, but they were no longer politically free: of 133 cardinals created by the popes of Avignon all but ten were Frenchmen. Money values dominated the curia in a degree never known in Rome, and the "Babylonian captivity" was harmful to the Church at large, while the absence of the popes from Italy meant that the Papal States fell apart in a welter of local wars. To make matters even worse, in 1348 Italy was swept by bubonic plague, the dreaded Black Death, which killed an estimated one third of the population.

In 1378 Pope Gregory XI, spurred on by the exhortations, the visions, and at times by the dire warnings, of two saintly women, Saint

The Byzantine emperor John Palaeologus sets sail for Venice in 1369 to beg the Doge for aid against Turkish attacks.

Bridget in Rome and Saint Catherine of Siena, and realizing that a return to Rome was imperative if he was to retain his temporal sovereignty over the Papal States, left Avignon by sea for Rome, where he arrived in January, 1377. When he died the following year, an Italian was elected pope as Urban VI, but Urban's election was contested by the French cardinals, who themselves elected a rival. The Great Western Schism had begun and was to last forty years: at one time there were no less than three rival popes. An end to the schism was finally made by the emperor. In 1417 Emperor Sigismund persuaded the cardinals to hold a council at Constance, on the border of Italy and Germany. There all three rival popes abdicated or were deposed and a new one was elected. A peaceful settlement to so embittered a controversy was a hopeful sign that statesmanship was replacing war and faction as a means of resolving disputes.

All through this troubled fourteenth century the city-states were growing in territory and power, usually under a despot, until, on the eve of the fifteenth century, there had emerged five principal states more or less equal in importance: Milan, Venice, Florence, the Papal States, and Naples. The duchy of Milan, nominally a fief of the empire, was in fact a despotism of the Visconti family, and its wealth came from trade and the manufacture of arms. The most important of the Visconti was Gian Galeazzo, so rich that he married the king of France's daughter. Ambitious to rule all Italy, Visconti had by 1400 extended his rule to Verona and Padua in the east, and south to Pisa and Siena.

Venice, still an oligarchy, kept aloof from Italian politics and concentrated her energy on increasing her already vast wealth. Twice a year her "Flanders galleys" set sail with a cargo of spices, sugar, pepper, and other Eastern products, by way of Gibraltar and Southampton to Bruges. Thence they returned with wood and furs from Scandinavia, English wool, Flemish cloth, and French wines. The Venetians turned their profits into the marble of fine public buildings: at this time Venice was the most beautiful city in Europe.

Florence was the only one of the Big Five to have a republican government. Her bankers handled the pope's finances, and were so rich they could afford to lend Edward III of England over a million florins to finance his wars, and to survive the king's failure to repay. But

Florence was threatened by Gian Galeazzo Visconti's seasoned troops, and in 1400 her chances of survival did not look very bright.

The Papal States, which during the Babylonian captivity had broken into small petty despotisms, were brought back to order by a strong Spaniard, Cardinal Albornoz. However, chaos again ensued during the Great Schism, and in 1400 the Papal States were the weakest of the Big Five. When the pope who had been elected at the Council of Constance arrived in Rome, there was hardly a city in the Papal States that acknowledged his right to rule.

Finally, Naples, by far the largest territory, since it occupied half of the peninsula, but also the most backward and poorest of the five, was ruled by an Angevin king, Ladislaus, in the autocratic tradition first imposed on this part of Italy by the Normans. Like Gian Galeazzo Visconti, Ladislaus made a bid to unite all Italy under his rule, and took advantage of the papal schism to seize the territory around Rome. But he lacked the wealth to keep a large army long in the field, and also, unlike Rome, Naples lacked the mystique that could rally non-Neapolitan Italians. The death of Ladislaus in 1414, wrote a contemporary Florentine, "brought release from fear and suspicion to Florence, and all other free cities of Italy." The failure of Ladislaus also made clear that during the *quattrocento* at least Italy would continue not as a united land but as a medley of city-states, some large, some small. The resultant diversity was in many respects to prove beneficial, since it made economic and cultural competition.

CHAPTER VI

THE EARLY RENAISSANCE

Florence in 1400 differed markedly from Italy's other major city-states. Strategically, it occupied a favorable position: far enough from the Alps not to be threatened by imperial armies, far enough from Rome to have escaped absorption by the Papal States. Protected by the Apennines, it could still communicate with the rest of Italy, and through the navigable Arno with the world at large. Because the surrounding soil was not rich, it had had to build up manufacturing. Its chief sources of wealth were woolen cloth, silk, and banking. Florentines invented the modern banking system: they had a network of branches and agents extending from London to Lübeck, and they were official bankers to the pope.

Business had left its mark on politics. Florence was a republic: out of a population of some fifty thousand men, women, and children, there were six thousand professionals and tradesmen who enjoyed citizenship and had a say in government—an unusually high proportion for the time. In foreign policy the merchants and bankers favored a policy of peace and trade which would continue to make the gold florin the strongest currency in Europe. Despite this international outlook,

Brunelleschi's dome crowns Santa Maria del Fiore Cathedral, Florence.

the Florentines were staunchly patriotic. They were proud of their republican system of government and were convinced that it was the system most conducive to personal freedom and well-being; they were prepared to defend it against any aggressor.

During the Dark and Middle Ages books had been the preserve of monks; the well-to-do laymen were soldiers with no time or taste for reading. But now in Florence there had arisen a new class of men with the leisure, education, and money to indulge a liking for books. Their tastes differed from the monks'. They wanted to read not about theology or saints' miraculous lives, but about men and women like themselves in recognizable situations. Of the old Latin authors they knew and appreciated Virgil, but the others, denounced as pagan and dangerous by the Church, had for centuries remained unread, and many were lost. Their reputation, however, lingered, and the educated laymen of Florence, believing these authors had much to teach, began to search for them in the monastery libraries of Europe.

The search proved fruitful beyond all expectation. Between 1400 and 1440 dozens of unknown works of Latin literature, and then of

The façade of the Medici bank in Milan is shown in a drawing by Filarete.

Greek literature, were found, mainly by Florentines. A Latin cookbook turned up in a Swiss monastery side by side with Lucretius' sublime philosophic poem *On the Nature of Things;* Cicero's letters to Atticus were found and revealed the writer not as the monk-like sage the Church had for centuries liked to imagine him, but as a staunch republican actively engaged in the defense of political liberty. Homer, Thucydides, and Plato became known. The wisdom and beauty of a thousand years were very quickly revealed, and all this chiefly in the small town of Florence.

The Florentines admired what they read, but naturally could not make use of all this treasure at once. Classical literature presents dozens of moral, philosophical, and political theories and many excellent types of behavior. It became necessary to select those elements that could be useful to them in their world as it was at the beginning of the fifteenth century. The Florentines selected three elements in particular.

The first thing that struck the Florentines was the immense impor-

INSET: *This medallion portraying the aged, gout-afflicted Cosimo de' Medici, called* Pater Patriae, *was struck shortly after his death.*

tance the Greeks and Romans had attached to will. Achilles and Odysseus, Alcibiades and the heroes sung by Pindar—each felt he must always excel and surpass himself, that a man wins his manhood through unflagging effort and unflinching risk. So too with the Romans, though more soberly—Scipio Africanus, Marius, Caesar, and countless others had forged their destinies through driving will. This impressed the Florentines all the more because they had been brought up on books like Boethius' *Consolations of Philosophy,* which put forth a world bristling with hostile forces, no good man able to cope, the only solution resignation, surrender of the will. Will to Christian authors usually meant God's will, and virtue consisted in complying with that. Since God's will was distressingly inscrutable, the result too often had been passivity, drift, and a static society.

The Florentines adopted the Roman name for this driving will, the power in a man that makes him what he is. They called it *virtus.* It differed from any Christian virtue, even from fortitude, for whereas fortitude is a kind of passive courage in the face of pain or adversity, *virtus* is positive and boundless. *Virtus* was the single most important element in the classical ideal evolved in Florence, and was to become the dynamism behind the city's future achievements.

The next characteristic which impressed the Florentines was the ancients' strong civil sense—their public-spiritedness—to be seen in Socrates' fighting barefoot through the winter campaign at Potidaea, Cicero's hurrying back from retirement to try to save the republic from Caesar, Pericles' adorning Athens with public buildings. This strengthened and extended in range the Florentines' own tradition of service. It helped end private vendettas, it led to patronage of artists, and to the sort of remark made by the architect Leon Battista Alberti, when he claimed that the design of the outside of a house was the most important, because it was the part all citizens could enjoy.

The third element selected by the Florentines for practical application was versatility. Whereas the Middle Ages had been a period of specialists based on the guild system, the ancients had tended to be all-rounders. Pericles had been not only a shrewd politician, but friend and patron of artists; Julius Caesar had been both general and historian; the elder Pliny had written on everything from painting to volcanoes. There had been no distinction then between clerics thinking

A detail from a fifteenth-century fresco by Ghirlandaio shows the Humanist scholar Angelo Poliziano (center) conversing with colleagues.

theoretical truths and laymen engaged in lower, practical concerns. Both pursuits were interrelated, for example, in Cicero. To critics who doubted his ability for philosophic writing after a lifelong political career, Cicero replied: "I have been studying philosophy most earnestly at the very time when I seemed to be doing so least." This reply became famous in Florence, with its implication that a man's thoughts and theories should grow out of practical experience. Such an approach was to become especially important in the arts. It did not escape notice that Socrates, as well as philosophizing, had earned his living as a sculptor—evidently a good one, for his "Three Graces" was kept in the Acropolis. Without the ideal of an artist who thinks, we might not have had the work of Leonardo da Vinci or Michelangelo.

Mainly from these elements the Florentines fashioned their ideal of a man strong-willed, public-spirited, versatile. Together with the Christian faith, this ideal was to produce Renaissance man. He was to achieve great things, first of all in Florence, whence his influence radiated. During the fifteenth century most of Italy was quickened by the Renaissance, but nowhere were the achievements so important as in Florence; it is fitting, therefore, to concentrate on that city.

The Florentines began the century with a great victory. Their city was besieged by Gian Galeazzo Visconti's large, well-armed Milanese army. Florence's neighbors hastily surrendered; many throughout Italy sincerely believed that the whole peninsula should be ruled by a single strong king, such as Gian Galeazzo. But the Florentines declined to believe this. They already saw themselves as upholders of republicanism, heirs of the ancient Romans, and they strengthened their morale by reading Cicero and Livy. They put up a long and extremely brave defense. In 1402 Gian Galeazzo suddenly died of a fever, and his great northern state split up. Florence found herself safe and still free.

The Florentines were now more than ever sure that "the ancients", on whom they had begun to model themselves held the key to success in every walk of life. In order to transmit the new classical learning, in 1428 the Florentines took a bold step. They altered that most conservative of systems, education, in order to give a prominent place to classical literature in the widest sense, including moral philosophy. They called the new course *litterae humaniores*—learning more humane than previous disciplines in that it dealt directly with human beings.

Six years later an even more important change took place when the
Florentines drove out Rinaldo degli Albizzi, an old-style leader who
believed that Florence should expand through war. As replacement,
they recalled from exile Cosimo de' Medici, a banker aged forty-five,
shrewd, well-educated, and humane, whose policy was peace. Florence
continued to be ruled by six priors, elected every two months, but behind the scenes Cosimo's moral authority was decisive. For the next two
generations, largely thanks to Cosimo's decision to form an alliance
with its traditional enemy Milan, Florence was able to enjoy peace.
That period of serenity was to make possible important achievements.

Cosimo was a warm admirer of classical learning. He collected the
best library in Florence and commissioned a doctor's son, Marsilio
Ficino, to translate Plato. But his particular interest was architecture.
During his exile he took with him his architect-friend Michelozzo
Michelozzi and had him draw the great buildings of Venice. Always
uneasy that he had amassed a fortune through moneylending, which
the Church denounced as usury, Cosimo on his return salved his conscience by building a new friary for the Dominicans. He knew the
recently discovered writings of the Roman architect Vitruvius and told
Michelozzo to design the friary with classical columns and round-
headed arches. Later he commissioned the church of San Spirito from
Filippo Brunelleschi, who had used ancient Roman techniques to construct a huge dome for Florence's cathedral.

Formerly, private houses had been plain fortress-like structures with
small windows and high towers from which to drive off possible as-
sailants. Cosimo commissioned Michelozzo to build him a house more
suited to the new age of peace in the now-fashionable classical style.
The resultant Palazzo Medici is a square building with round-headed
windows and the bold cornice which had been a feature of houses in
ancient Rome. In the interior is a courtyard flanked by classical columns
and decorated with bas-reliefs copied from the ancients.

To grace the courtyard of this unusual house Cosimo commissioned
from his friend Donatello an unusual statue. David who had slain
Goliath had long been considered by Florentines as a symbol of their
own republic which, though comparatively small, had maintained its
independence against larger aggressive monarchies. David in the past
had always been depicted clothed, but now, so strong was enthusiasm

OVERLEAF: *The fanciful "Rout of San Romano" by Paolo Uccello was commissioned in the fifteenth century for the Medici palace.*

for all things classical that Cosimo requested Donatello to portray David in the nude, as the Greeks had depicted their heroes and gods. The result was the first nude statue in the round since the days of ancient Rome, a bronze of great intrinsic beauty which was also to become one of the most influential works in the history of art.

Under Cosimo's guidance Florence prospered and became famous for her new ideas, new wealth, and new buildings. When Cosimo died in 1464 the Florentines accorded him the title of *Pater Patriae,* Father of his Country, and continued the system he had evolved by allowing first his son, then his grandson Lorenzo to continue as leading citizen. Lorenzo's leadership lasted from 1469 to 1492. He had exactly the same rights as other citizens, but his moral authority was greater than theirs, partly because he bore the by now famous name of Medici, partly because of his own brilliantly magnanimous personality, which won him the sobriquet Magnificent.

Lorenzo was so brimful of energy, talent, and warmth that people hardly noticed his homeliness—his flattened nose, jutting underlip, and narrow eyes. In his life he combined in rich measure the three elements of the classical ideal. Though he would have liked to live quietly in the country writing nature poetry, he chose to serve his city as a statesman, successfully guiding Florence through a dangerous quarrel with Pope Sixtus IV over a frontier dispute. During that quarrel the city exchequer was exhausted; Lorenzo showed his public-spiritedness by selling one of his estates in order to pay the troops. As for versatility, Lorenzo proved his worth as banker, politician, farmer, breeder of race horses, patron of the arts, philosopher, writer of religious lyrics and of bawdy carnival songs.

Lorenzo was very friendly with his grandfather's protégé, Marsilio Ficino, a priest of diminutive stature and giant intelligence. Both hero-worshiped Plato and they decided to found a society of Platonists, calling it the Academy, which was the name Plato had given to his own school. The Academy met regularly to discuss topics arising from Plato's *Dialogues,* and dined together annually on Plato's birthday.

The main object of the Academy, which gathered all the leading thinkers in Florence, was to harmonize the Christian religion with classical wisdom. It troubled the Florentines that the ancient Egyptians, Greeks, and Romans should have evolved religious systems in which

"David," the first free-standing nude sculpture done since ancient times, was fashioned in bronze by Donatello.

there was a Creator, and sometimes a trinity of supreme gods, as well as codes of ethics which set high value on generosity and unselfishness. How, they asked, had the pagan Socrates found strength to die in the cause of truth, almost like a Christian martyr? Was the Church correct in stating that Christianity had a monopoly of grace and truth? If so, how to explain such heroic behavior and so many intellectual insights?

Led by Ficino, the Academy answered these questions rather as the early Church fathers had dealt with the undoubted truths and personal holiness to be found in the Old Testament. They evolved a theory of foreshadowing. They argued that God had allowed the human intelligence, even unaided by grace, to foresee dimly some of the supernatural truths later to be revealed by Jesus Christ, and so to pave the way for the acceptance of Christianity. If the Greeks held that their hero Perseus was born of a virgin, that was because they dimly appre-

hended the truth of the Incarnation, even before it was revealed.

The theory of foreshadowing had important results. Instead of being treated as outcasts, the pre-Christian thinkers were now looked upon as friends and allies in a centuries-old quest for truth. There arose in Florence a sense of a common humanity with men of all places and all epochs. When Pope Pius II came to ask Cosimo de' Medici for money and ships to launch a new crusade against the Turk, his request fell on deaf ears. The Florentines were no longer interested in ideological wars; they preferred to seek reconciliation, and it was at the Council of Florence, in 1439, that the centuries-old division between the Roman and Greek Churches was temporarily healed.

Members of the Academy liked to identify themselves and their friends with famous men of antiquity. Ficino called himself Plato reborn, while Botticelli was identified with the great Greek draughtsman,

Botticelli's "Mars and Venus" was inspired by a poem by Lucretius, a first-century B.C. *philosopher and poet.*

Apelles. Botticelli even chose some of his subjects because they were known to have been painted by Apelles. In other pictures, Botticelli illustrated the Academy's doctrine of the foreshadowing of Christianity. In his "Birth of Venus" winged zephyrs, the classical equivalent of angels, waft the sea-born goddess to shore on a scallop shell, Christian symbol of baptism and regeneration. Venus rises from the sea, as Christ rose from His baptism in the Jordan, and is given a garment by a nymph, as Noah was clothed by his sons.

In his earlier "Primavera," Botticelli's immediate subject is spring, the season of love. Venus is with child, a warm wind stirs flowers to life, the Three Graces dance joyfully, and one of them, touched by Cupid, turns toward Mercury. But Botticelli's conception of spring is the reverse of pagan. Venus extends her hand to modulate the Graces' dance; Mercury is not merely a handsome youth but a revealer of truth as he touches the clouds to unveil the mysteries beyond. The deeper message of the "Primavera" is this: While spring wakens the world to beauty, Venus uses love to turn the human heart to truths divine.

The Medici were connoisseurs and patrons of art. Cosimo had befriended Donatello—who, on his deathbed, asked to be buried beside the banker-statesman—as well as the painters Fra Angelico and Fra Filippo Lippi. Cosimo's son Piero had commissioned battle scenes from a mosaicist turned painter, Paolo Uccello, and had also considerably enlarged the family collection of *objets d'art* and ancient statuary. It was Lorenzo, characteristically openhanded, who put that collection on public display in the garden of the Palazzo Medici, thus constituting the first museum of modern times. Lorenzo also opened a school of sculpture, where promising youths studied classical models.

Michelangelo entered that school at the age probably of thirteen. Lorenzo allowed him to eat at his table and treated the artist as one of his sons. One day another protégé of Lorenzo's, the poet Angelo Poliziano, suggested to Michelangelo that the battle of centaurs described in one of Ovid's poems would make a good subject for a bas-relief. Michelangelo took the poet's advice and produced his earliest masterpiece, a work in which nude muscular figures lunge, strain, and writhe. Never before had an artist so convincingly depicted human energy, but this was not a chance happening or even just an expression of Michelangelo's temperament. It was the visual representation of the classical concept of *virtus*. Lorenzo's friend Leon Battista Alberti expressed it thus: "Men can do anything with themselves if they will."

Side by side with philosophical speculation and great art went advances in science. It was the Tuscan, Leonardo Fibonacci, who had first replaced Roman numerals by the less cumbersome Arabic numerals, and a Florentine, Paolo Toscanelli, by profession a doctor, who first scientifically plotted the course of the comet later known as Halley's comet. At the Council of Florence, called to heal the split between Eastern and Western Christianity, Toscanelli questioned Eastern delegates about the geography of the Black Sea region and concluded that Asia occupied a much greater expanse of the globe than ancient writers had believed. Hence the Atlantic was less wide than was generally supposed and could be navigated in existing ships. When Columbus began to plan his voyage to the land he supposed to be Cathay, he wrote for advice to the Florentine. Toscanelli expounded his ideas in a letter and sent Columbus a map in which he represented the Atlantic as 2,500 miles wide, not far from its true proportions. Columbus carried the letter and the map with him on the voyage in which he discovered the New World. Later another Florentine, Amerigo Vespucci, a former employee of the Medici bank, continued Columbus' explorations and gave his own name to the new continents.

By the last decade of the fifteenth century Florence had grown in size and beauty and in every branch of intellectual achievement. New churches, private houses, and public buildings had arisen; their walls were hung with paintings in which, thanks to the use of perspective— another Florentine invention—people and objects appeared almost three-dimensional. Two printing presses produced books which all could afford, whereas a hundred years earlier manuscripts had been the privilege of the rich few; it had become fashionable to be well educated —there were some Florentine women who could speak classical Greek. Ficino considered recent decades an age of gold. But the Florentines did not give themselves all the credit for their achievements. Just as Ficino prided himself not on being an original thinker but on reincarnating the spirit of Plato, so the Florentines prided themselves on reincarnating the greatness of the past. The first use of the Renaissance metaphor occurs in a treatise by the Florentine architect, Filarete. After describing a modern town much like his own, with stone houses and

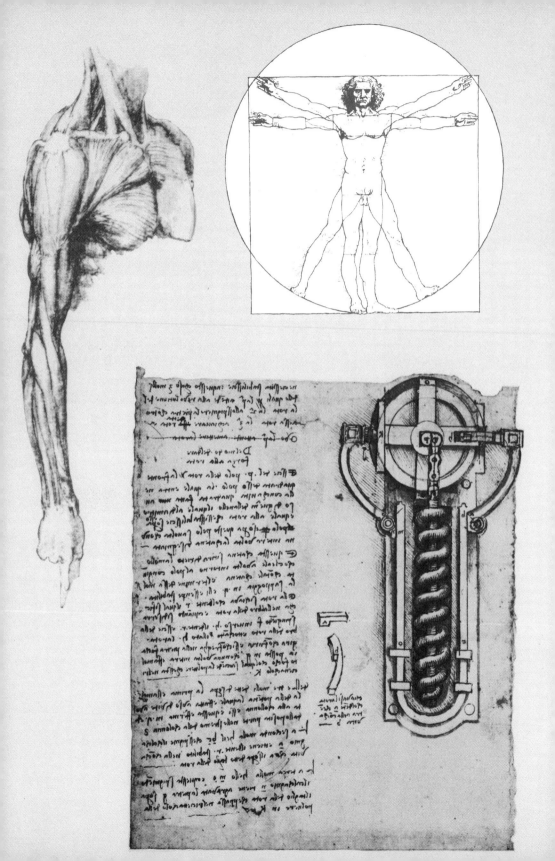

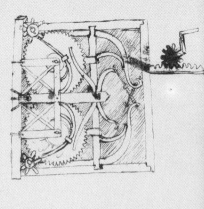

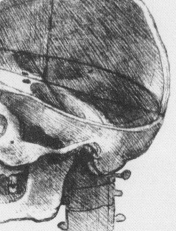

The broad scope of Leonardo da Vinci's imagination can be seen in this selection of drawings from his notebooks. Top, far left to right: anatomical study of an arm, the proportions of the body, the flower star-of-Bethlehem, an automobile propelled by springs. Bottom, far left to right: a flint-lock mechanism, a human skull, and a face.

broad streets watered by fountains, he has someone say admiringly: "I seem to see again the noble buildings that were once in Rome and those that we read were in Egypt. It seems to me that on seeing those noble buildings I have been reborn—*mi pare rinascere.*"

The Florentines not only initiated the Renaissance, they carried it to other parts of Italy. In nearby Urbino, Duke Federigo da Montefeltro, an invincible *condottiere* who had been employed by Florence, filled his tiny court with scholars and artists, including the Tuscan Piero della Francesca, and kept thirty scribes busy copying classics for his library. In Mantua, Poliziano's *Orfeo,* Europe's first lyric drama, was staged in 1471, while Ferrara dramatists pioneered elaborate productions, in Italian, of the plays by Plautus and Terence which Florentine scholars had rediscovered in cobwebbed monastery libraries. To Lodovico Sforza's court at Milan Leonardo da Vinci carried the Florentine sytle of painting and his own brilliant inventions. There he painted a portrait of Lodovico's young mistress, Cecilia Gallerani, fondling an ermine, and his immense fresco of "The Last Supper"; he devised war machines and installed a pump for the duchess' bath; he mounted colorful spectacles to distract the court and cudgeled his brain for ways of making an immense hundred-ton bronze horse. He made a model for it, but like so many of Leonardo's projects, the horse and rider were never realized.

Not everyone in Florence approved of these new achievements within and without the city. A gloomy Dominican, Girolamo Savonarola, born in Ferrara but resident in Cosimo's foundation of San Marco, protested against the bankers' wealth and their wives' low-cut dresses and cosmetics; he castigated as unholy the Academy's esteem for Plato and artists' portrayal of nudes; more generally he denounced as an abomination the whole idea of turning life, which the Church had traditionally viewed as a vale of tears, into a gay, even daring attempt at self-fulfillment and discovery.

Lorenzo tried to appease Savonarola with generous gifts of alms, but the Dominican was not one to compromise—his reason for becoming a friar was that he "could not endure the enormous wickedness of the blinded people of Italy"—and anyway the ideological differences were probably too wide to be bridged. The century was nearing its end and Savonarola traded on the fears which swept Italians at such times to preach a series of apocalyptic sermons, prophesying that unless the Florentines repented and turned their backs on pagan pleasures, their city would be destroyed by fire. He hinted even at a foreign invasion. So persuasive was the friar's oratory and so ingrained the people's fear of hell-fire that a mass repentance swept the city. Twelve thousand at a time crowded to hear Savonarola thunder; many including Michelangelo wept, and Botticelli swore to paint no more nudes.

In 1492 Lorenzo died and was succeeded as first citizen by his son Piero. An immature youth of twenty-one, Piero lacked his father's winning charm and gave himself airs. For almost two centuries Italy had been mercifully free from foreign invasion, but now the ambitious young king of France, Charles VIII, decided to press a flimsy claim to the kingdom of Naples, which had once been ruled by his Angevin kinsmen. With an army of ten thousand men—larger by far than any force an Italian state could muster—and forty cannon, Charles VIII crossed the Alps in 1494 as the ally of Milan, while Florence, Naples, and the papacy combined to resist his coming. That winter Charles marched across the Apennines toward Florence. Piero grew frightened, hurried to parley with him, and weakly yielded Tuscan garrison towns without adequate guarantee. When he rode home, the Florentines, furious at his foolish conduct, forced him and his brother Giovanni—the future Leo X—into exile. The king of France made his headquarters in the Palazzo Medici, while his officers commandeered the most comfortable houses as billets.

The French stayed only a week or so in Florence before marching south to occupy Naples, and the following year, having overextended their lines of communication and alienated their ally, Milan, they were obliged to withdraw altogether from Italy. But the shock for Florence was severe and lasting. The city's wonderful achievements were seen to be flimsy so long as they could not be defended against an aggressor. Savonarola's prophecy had come true, and in a hysteria of repentance the Florentines gave political power to Savonarola. The Dominican reorganized Florence as an oligarchy, led penitential processions, declared half the days of the year fast days—thereby provoking protests from the butchers—and built bonfires on which were burned cosmetics, musical instruments, so-called indecent books and paintings.

Savonarola had always believed that Florence could be a center of

regeneration for Italy. Not content with turning Florence into what he termed a Christian theocracy, he began to denounce Rome, then at a very low moral ebb under the Spanish Borgia pope, Alexander VI. "In the early Church," cried Savonarola, "the chalices were of wood, the prelates of gold; in these days the Church has chalices of gold and prelates of wood." As the friar stepped up his attacks, Alexander excommunicated him. When Savonarola continued to say Mass, Alexander placed Florence under an interdict. This was to use temporal arms in a spiritual battle, for it meant that Florentine goods in Rome and elsewhere could be confiscated. As the Florentines began to feel the economic pinch, Savonarola lost favor. In a last effort to assert his power, one of the friar's colleagues boasted that Savonarola would walk across a burning pyre carrying the Blessed Sacrament. The challenge was taken up, a pyre built and lighted, but at the last moment Savonarola refused to enter the flames. The Florentines rounded on their former hero; seizing him they tortured him into a series of confessions. In 1498 he was hanged and burned in the main square, where so much Florentine beauty had gone up in flames, and his ashes were scattered on the waters of the Arno.

Analyzing Florence's ignominious occupation by the French, Machiavelli claimed that the basic mistake had been the failure to organize the citizens in a well-trained militia. Machiavelli was probably right. But it had been a cardinal point in Florentine statecraft ever since the civil wars of the Middle Ages that to give arms to the people spelled anarchy. The Florentines had devoted all their energies to the arts of peace, forgetting that they lived not in the days of Plato or Cicero but in a harsh new world of powerful nation-states, where a small people had to pay particular attention to defense.

The Florentines never properly recovered from the occupation of 1494, or from the tragic failure of Savonarola. Economically the city had already begun to decline, as English and Flemish textiles ousted Florentine scarlet cloth from traditional markets. The Florentines had made their unique and immensely important contribution to civilization. As though they realized that their task was complete, energy and patriotism waned, and it is no accident that their most promising artist, Michelangelo, was to emigrate to Rome, which, with the beginning of a new century, succeeded Florence as the center of Italy.

An anonymous painting shows the death of Savonarola, who was hanged and then burned in the Piazza della Signoria, Florence, on May 23, 1498.

CHAPTER VII

THE LATER RENAISSANCE

Rome in 1500 was a city so poor and run-down that the Romans of Augustus Caesar's day would probably not have recognized it. Cattle grazed in the Forum, the Colosseum housed squalid taverns and shops; thieves infested the ancient baths, and in the filthy alleys during the three months preceding Alexander VI's coronation 220 murders were committed. A population of forty thousand were notoriously idle and produced no top-quality goods; some provided for or served the papal court, others kept inns or lodgings for the many pilgrims and lawyers who came to Rome on Church business. There were only a few signs of the new classical enlightenment: a library formed by the Tuscan pope, Nicholas V; and the Sistine Chapel, its vault still undecorated, built by Sixtus IV, the pope who had made war on Florence. But by and large the city and its inhabitants were undistinguished. There were no well-known Roman thinkers, writers, or artists, and the immoral Spanish-born pope, Alexander VI, had hardly helped civilize his capital by introducing the bullfight and spending pilgrims' offerings on a dukedom for his son Cesare Borgia—the ferocious but much admired model for Machiavelli's *The Prince*.

Designed by Bernini, the interior of the dome of Saint Peter's is 390 feet high. Sixteen windows illuminate its mosaic panels.

When he died in 1503, Alexander's bloated, blackened body was unceremoniously buried to the accompaniment of jeering workmen, and in one of the shortest conclaves ever held the cardinals elected Alexander's sternest critic, Giuliano della Rovere, a blunt, self-willed, pugnacious Ligurian. By this time a new French king, Louis XII, had invaded Italy, seized the duchy of Milan, divided the kingdom of Naples with Spain, and, in alliance with Venice, was threatening the Romagna, one of the Papal States. The new pope was determined to safeguard the States of the Church, and as the surest means of doing so swore to drive the barbarian, as he termed King Louis of France, from Italian soil. It was almost certainly in allusion to Julius Caesar that he took the name Julius II.

Pope Julius' line of thought stemmed from an influential book, *Decades,* written in 1460 by a papal employee, Flavius Blondus. Blondus argued that the popes are the rightful successors of the Roman emperors and, under the new Christian dispensation, are called to revive the ancient glory of Rome. It was a heady doctrine, destined to revive Roman morale after centuries of war and desolation, but dangerous also in that the popes tended to see the new classical learning in terms of self-aggrandizement. Whereas the Florentines had considered themselves heirs of the Roman Republic, and therefore upholders of personal liberty and free speech, the Romans lauded the empire, when one man's word had been law.

Julius soon showed that he meant to live up to his name. When Perugia and Bologna rose in revolt, he put himself at the head of an army and recaptured both towns. Again in the winter of 1510–11 Julius, now aged sixty-seven, donned his armor to march against Duke Alfonso d'Este of Ferrara, an ally of France. Julius' army occupied Modena and besieged Mirandola, the gateway to Ferrara. It was a bitter winter and Julius was prostrated with fever. But he roused himself from his sickbed to tour the lines wearing a fur coat and looking like a bear. "He goes about in all the weather . . . ," wrote the Venetian envoy, "he has the strength of a giant. . . . His court, who have no heart for Italy, and think of nothing but their money, are dying to get back to Rome; but they are quite helpless; Julius II thinks, dreams and talks . . . of nothing but Mirandola." When the town fell, the impatient Pope Julius would not wait for his soldiers to open the gates to the city but climbed over the wall on a scaling ladder.

As well as being warriors the Roman emperors had been large-scale builders, and here also Julius pursued the classical ideal. Saint Peter's was twelve centuries old and its south wall in danger of collapse. Its dim interior, wooden ceiling, and Byzantine-style mosaics excited scorn in an age which had come to esteem only classical architecture. In 1506 Julius ordered the old church demolished and himself laid the foundation of a vast new basilica designed by Bramante. He chose the form of a Greek cross and crowned it with a dome like that of the Pantheon, the only temple from ancient times still extant in Rome. Julius set an army of builders to work, but the undertaking was so enormous that it would take more than a century to complete.

In 1504 Julius summoned Michelangelo to Rome. The Florentine sculptor was then twenty-nine and had already made his name with a statue of the Blessed Virgin holding the dead Christ in her arms, and another statue, fourteen feet high, of David. Julius commissioned Michelangelo to make a tomb for him—no ordinary tomb but a huge freestanding, three-tier mausoleum adorned with forty large marble figures. Michelangelo warmed to the scheme and went to Carrara personally to choose the finest white marble. Soon the blocks began to pile up in the piazza outside Saint Peter's, but by then the pope's enthusiasm for the tomb had cooled. He had won military successes and his plans now centered less on his own death than on the embellishment of Rome. Julius invited Michelangelo to fresco the ceiling of his uncle's Sistine Chapel. Michelangelo, who wanted to finish the tomb, protested that he was a sculptor, not a painter; indeed he had never tried fresco before. But Julius insisted, and his will proved stronger even than Michelangelo's.

It took Michelangelo four years to fresco the vast ceiling, 133 by 43 feet. Constantly starved of money to buy paints, more than once he had to travel far to implore Julius for funds. The nine main scenes, taken from Genesis, begin with the creation of the world and continue to the last years of Noah. In the frames surrounding these scenes are seated nude youths, probably symbolizing Greek and Roman man. On the border are the prophets and sibyls who foresaw the Incarnation, and the ancestors of Christ, waiting in dark expectancy for the event which was to change the destiny of man, and which, on the altar below,

at Mass, was daily re-enacted. The whole is a panorama of pre-Christian history viewed as a foreshadowing of Christian redemption.

Not content with employing one genius, Julius called in a second: twenty-five-year-old Raphael, born in Urbino, trained in Florence. Raphael's greatest work for Julius is the Stanza della Segnatura, housing the pope's private library in the Vatican. Here he painted on one wall the culmination of pagan philosophy, "The School of Athens," dominated by the figure of Plato pointing heavenward; and on the wall opposite, the culmination of Christian faith, which completes and perfects the teaching of the noblest Greeks: "The Dispute on the Sacrament," surrounded by Doctors of the Church—Jerome, Augustine, Gregory, and Ambrose.

Julius laid broad new streets through the city of Rome—one of them, the Via Giulia, still bears his name—and began the Vatican Museum by acquiring the newly unearthed classical statuary "Apollo Belvedere" and "Laocoön." After his victories Julius was hailed by the Romans as a new Caesar. In fact his military successes were minor and when he came to die in 1513, the French were still in Milan, and the Spaniards were beginning to spread north from Naples. Nevertheless, Julius did set a new stamp on the papacy, and on Italy. He showed that he intended the papacy to remain a strong independent force even in the new age of nation-states. And he began to modernize Rome as a visible sign of the Church's spiritual authority.

Julius was succeeded by Lorenzo de' Medici's son Giovanni, who took the name Leo X. Again the name is significant, for an earlier Leo had deterred Attila from sacking Rome: the fear now was not only of France, but also of Spain and Germany. To deter new Attilas, Leo used diplomacy, not war, and his friends murmured admiringly: "After Caesar, Augustus." Leo was portly and shortsighted; he liked hunting and witty conversation; and he showed himself a true Medici in his taste for classical Latin, for poetry, and for gently beautiful pictures. His first act as pope was to appoint as his secretaries two accomplished Latin writers, Pietro Bembo and Jacopo Sadoleto, who were told to conduct the international correspondence of the Church in the Ciceronian mode.

Leo continued the building of Saint Peter's. Michelangelo was too dynamic for his taste, but he did employ Raphael not only in the papal

Cesare Borgia, son of Pope Alexander VI, was a brilliant but ruthless leader whose political maneuvers were immortalized in Machiavelli's The Prince.

apartments but in making a series of tapestries for the Sistine Chapel, the masterly cartoons of which have been preserved, though the tapestries were destroyed. Leo lavished money on a swarm of poets and he patronized the theater. Among the plays he attended was Machiavelli's cynical *Mandragola,* in which one of the characters is a wholly amoral priest. Leo's playgoing shocked Germans at the papal court, but one of Leo's spokesmen explained that Roman emperors such as Trajan had patronized the theater: the implication was that a pope might do whatever had been sanctioned by the emperors.

When a young German priest named Martin Luther visited Rome in 1511, he was dismayed at the way priests raced through Mass and by the general lack of spirituality. Romans seemed to him to care more for Aristotle than for the Gospels. He was partly right. Leo and his friends, following Julius' lead, were making an immense effort to repair centuries of material neglect and intellectual stagnation. They wished the capital of Christendom to take the lead in expounding a new way of life combining all that was best in the classical past with Christianity. To that end no expense was spared. For example, Leo, a connoisseur of music, spent lavishly on lutanists and singers to chant Mass in the chapel where Michelangelo's ceiling and Raphael's tapestries glowed in their pristine splendor.

Saint Peter's in particular was costing huge sums. It was common practice to offer an indulgence to anyone who would contribute to a church building fund, and in 1516 Leo instituted the indulgence in Germany to aid Saint Peter's. One of the agents who preached the indulgence was the friar Johann Tetzel, who asserted, "As soon as coin in the coffer rings, the soul from purgatory springs." "If the pope knew the exactions of these ventors," Luther commented, "he would rather Saint Peter's should lie in ashes than . . . be built of the blood and hide of the sheep." Luther maintained that the whole idea of buying forgiveness was contrary to the Gospel and from there went on to proclaim that God demands no good works on man's part; man must simply accept God's mercy, given through Christ, in a spirit of humility, faith, and trust.

For two reasons Leo was unfitted to come to terms with the contentious German monk. First, he had received no training in theology, and was dependent on the advice of hidebound experts less humane than he. Secondly, the emulation of Roman emperors had had a poisonous effect; on one occasion Leo refused to go into mourning for a Medici kinsman because, he announced, he was not like other men, but "a demigod"—thus claiming for himself a rank of which certain Roman emperors had habitually boasted. While his agents showered insults on Luther, Leo condemned the Ninety-five Theses out of hand. Luther countered by challenging the authority of popes and even of Church councils, claiming Scripture as his sole authority. In 1520 Leo excommunicated Luther. But that did not silence the forceful rebel. Luther burned the papal bull and continued to write blistering tracts that enjoyed a wide sale: he urged a return to the simplicity of the early Church and denied the doctrine of transubstantiation. Leo died in 1521 blissfully unaware that Luther's attacks, coupled with age-old German grievances against Rome, were to cost the Church much of Europe. He and his advisers were almost completely immersed in the classical past and out of touch with the spirit of nationalism rising beyond the Alps.

Leo was succeeded by his cousin Giulio de' Medici, who took the name Clement VII. A lesser man than his predecessors, Clement found it always difficult and often impossible to decide on a definite course of action. Northern Italy had now become the scene of a war between King Francis I of France and the Holy Roman Emperor Charles V, ruler not only of the imperial possessions in Germany but also of Spain and of Spanish overseas dominions, including Naples. Clement promised support first to one, then to the other, and succeeded only in alienating both.

In 1527 Charles' army of Germans and Spaniards were rebellious and unpaid, the emperor himself being absent in Spain. Many of the German troops were Lutherans; they saw Rome as a new Babylon and the pope as anti-Christ. All the soldiers were aware of the immense wealth accumulated in Rome by recent popes. That spring an unruly horde of troops commanded by a renegade Frenchman, the duke of Bourbon, marched south from Piacenza, and one misty May morning scaled the low walls hemming the Vatican hill. Clement fled with three thousand followers, including his goldsmith Benvenuto Cellini, to the Castel Sant' Angelo. The horde swept into the city. While Lutherans sacked churches and, putting on priestly vestments, parodied the ac-

OVERLEAF: *The Grand Canal in Venice provides the setting for Carpaccio's "Healing of the Demoniac," seen on an upper balcony.*

tions of the Mass, Spaniards looted, tortured, and raped. Two out of three houses in Rome were burned and priceless works of art destroyed. Only in December did Clement succeed in raising the huge sum demanded for his surety and slip out of his ruined capital.

In 1529 Clement, Francis, and Charles concluded a treaty which was to give Italy peace and a new order. The Treaty of Cambrai confirmed the permanent presence in Italy of the foreigner and so spelled out the bankruptcy of papal policy as initiated by Julius II. Francis I gave up his claim to Milan, which six years later came to be ruled by a Spanish viceroy; Clement acknowledged Charles as ruler of Naples. In return he was allowed to keep the Papal States intact and was promised imperial troops to restore his relatives in Florence, which was accomplished after some fierce fighting. Charles bound the minor Italian states to his banner by marriages or military aid and thus in the mid-1530s found himself the arbiter of Italy.

Machiavelli in *The Prince* had urged the Medici to unite the main Italian states and free the whole peninsula from Frenchmen and Spaniards. To this end Machiavelli counselled unscrupulous cunning, hypocrisy, murder if necessary, and above all tough troops possessing animal ferocity: "There are two methods of fighting, the one by law, the other by force: the first method is that of men, the second of beasts; but as the first is often insufficient, one must have recourse to the second." The Christian religion, Machiavelli believed, had sapped Italian virility and he, like so many thinkers of his day, was really looking to a pre-Christian past for the impetus and techniques to drive out the foreigner.

Machiavelli is often praised as a realist, but in fact his advice in *The Prince* was in the circumstances wholly unrealistic. Italians had lost their skill in warfare and local rivalries loomed far larger than any common hatred of the foreigner. Even if Italians had been capable of burying their differences it is doubtful whether they would have been able to defeat Frenchmen, Germans, and Spaniards, all with a long unbroken tradition of soldiering. Furthermore, Italians lacked a leader. Rome was the only city that could concentrate loyalties, but the popes, almost by definition, were men of peace who sought to reconcile differences (Julius is the exception who proves the rule). Even when obliged to fight they were thinking of peace terms; and they were bound to be

Raphael flattered his patron, Julius II, by using his features and the faces of court members in a painting of Gregory IX and Saint Raymond.

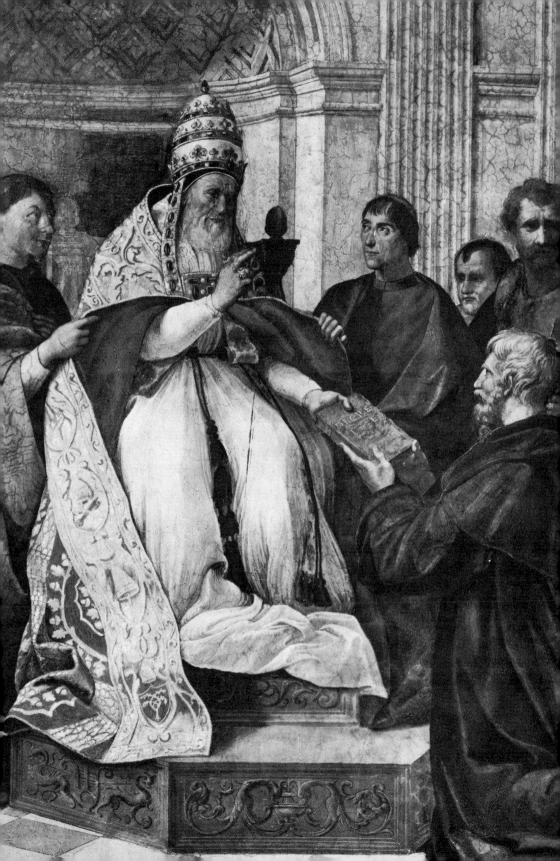

more concerned about the integrity of the Papal States than the welfare of Italy as a whole.

The sack of Rome virtually ended the Renaissance in Rome, in the sense that Romans no longer believed that by effort and the application of classical learning they could achieve remarkable results. The mood of hope and receptiveness was burned out by the looting invaders, to be replaced by weariness and fear; 1542 is a significant date, for in that year Pope Paul III established the Roman Inquisition in imitation of the medieval Inquisition in force in Spain. Indeed, as Spain's political power increased, the reactionary values of Spain began to become dominant in Rome.

The Renaissance which had started in Florence and then found its chief impetus in Rome sought refuge in Venice after the sack. The lagoon city had long kept apart from the mainstream of Italian life. The merchants of Venice had closer dealings with Mainz and Constantinople than with Naples or Rome. Their buildings were Gothic and Byzantine; their oligarchy, based exclusively on a stud book in which the marriages and births of those with blue blood were carefully entered, had nothing in common with the republics, despotisms, and princedoms of the rest of Italy; and as for the Church, the Venetians insisted that clerics, like other citizens, must stand trial for any crime before a civil, not a Church, court. In no city was the power of the state so complete; yet because of her mercantile traditions there was a long, proud tradition of tolerance. Tolerance was a virtue of which Italy now stood in pressing need.

The Venetian Republic extended on the mainland as far west as Verona, and across the Adriatic to the Dalmatian Coast in what is now Yugoslavia. Knowing that their frontiers were vulnerable and recognizing, as other Italian states did not, that war with one of the powerful new nations would mean defeat and an end of independence, the Venetians perfected a policy of survival through diplomacy. Their ambassadors worked night and day watching every political move and reporting them with minute detail in letters that still provide the best picture of sixteenth-century Europe. When a prince or politician who could be useful to Venice visited the lagoon city he was welcomed by the silk-gowned senators in their state barges and by uniformed musicians; he was feasted at a state banquet which ended with decorative

An afternoon haze settles over the town of Orvieto and its majestic cathedral.

statues of sugar candy fashioned by famous artists; his bedroom was lined with velvet and the best paintings; he was honored with a fireworks display and offered one of the city's courtesans—there were 11,654 out of a population of 150,000; and he was shown the arsenal, which by methods resembling mass production turned out a galley a day. Henry III of France remembered his state visit for the rest of his life, as did other dignitaries: they helped spread the word that Venice was still rich, still powerful, though, as the Venetian senators knew only too well, the republic's trade was declining because of the newly discovered ocean routes, and Venice was living on ancestral wealth.

To this independent and tolerant city, after the sack of Rome, trooped a number of gifted Italians. The one who got himself talked about most was Pietro Aretino. A Tuscan from Arezzo, son of a painter and a prostitute, Pietro was a big zestful man who reveled in the color and bustle he could see from his house on the Grand Canal. He wrote pornographic poems and tragedies based on Roman history, but his most important contribution to his times was a series of open letters— in effect an early form of newspaper—addressed to notable men in which he heaped witty abuse on any tyrannical action and rhapsodized on generosity, tolerance, and mercy. Aretino became such an influential figure that he was wooed with gifts of money by princes and others with some dark deed to hide, knowing full well that unless they paid up they would be pilloried by the "Scourge of Princes." "The alchemy of my pen," Aretino boasted, "has drawn over 25,000 crowns from the entrails of various princes"—including Henry VIII of England. However, Aretino was not always successful. He suggested to Michelangelo that a gift of one of the artist's valuable drawings would not come amiss. When his hint was ignored, Aretino roundly abused Michelangelo's style of art. The Florentine took his revenge when he came to paint "The Last Judgment" for the wall of the Sistine Chapel: he gave Saint Bartholomew the features of Aretino, while the flayed skin the saint dangles wears the face of his victim, Michelangelo.

Among Aretino's friends was the Florentine sculptor and architect Jacopo Sansovino. He too settled in Venice and built a dozen edifices in the classical style, notably the old library in the Piazza San Marco. When a workman's negligence caused the roof of the partly completed library to collapse, the angry government threw Sansovino into prison;

it was Aretino and another of Aretino's friends, Titian, who came to the rescue and got the unfortunate architect off with a light fine.

The architect who imprinted the Renaissance style most widely on the Venetian Republic was Andrea Palladio of Vicenza. Of humble birth, he was working as a mason when a rich Venetian scholar, Giangiorgio Trissino, discovered the youth's gift for mathematics and took him to Rome to study ancient buildings. From what he saw and from reading the ancient treatise of Vitruvius, who insisted that the proportions of each room must be related to the dimensions of the whole, Palladio devised a style whereby certain features of classical Roman art were applied to the building of churches and private houses. The best of Palladio's churches is San Giorgio Maggiore, far out on the edge of the lagoon. His country houses, or villas, were mainly designed for rich Venetians who had withdrawn their money from declining commerce to invest in mainland estates. Though the Venetians liked to think they were living in just the sort of house that Cicero or Pliny had inhabited, Palladio's villas were in fact very different from their ancient Roman counterparts. They lacked the central courtyard, and the pedimented portico framing the main entrance was a distinctive feature of temples such as the Pantheon, but never of domestic architecture. Nevertheless, Palladio's harmonious houses have the touch of genius and rank among the most influential achievements of the Renaissance.

Venetian painters liked to crowd their canvases with bejeweled figures clad in silk and velvet, supping, drinking, and enjoying life to the full in gilded rooms richly furnished with lush carpets, silk hangings, and heavy tapestries. They depicted women full-bodied and pearl-fleshed—as Venetian women probably were in real life, for the absence of roads and gardens made it difficult to take exercise or to sit out in the sunshine. Paolo Veronese excelled at these pictorial cornucopias—visual equivalents of the Rialto heaped with merchandise—and even introduced them into a Last Supper. Inquisitors demanded that Veronese remove the "buffoons, drunkards, Germans, dwarfs, and similar indecencies" from so holy a scene. Quick-tempered Michelangelo would have stormed out of the city, refusing to alter a brush stroke, but the Venetians were suppler than the Florentines and perhaps more cunning: Veronese satisfied the Inquisitors—less suspicious than their counterparts in Rome—simply by changing his picture's title to "Ban-

The nude came to Venice by way of Cardinal Bembo, one of Leo's secretaries, but also love-poet, Platonist, and collector. Among the statues in Bembo's collection was a Venus by or copied from Praxiteles. This work attracted the attention of Bembo's young protégé, Giorgione, who had the original idea of depicting a Venus, with classical proportions similar to that of the statue, reclining asleep in a peaceful countryside. Giorgione's "Sleeping Venus" introduced to European painting not only the reclining figure but also a new mood: the harmony between human beauty and landscape.

A rugged mountaineer from the Dolomites, Titian continued to work the seam opened up by Giorgione, but instead of delicate poetry his mood was exuberant and sometimes frankly sensuous. Perhaps his most characteristic work is the "Bacchanal," in which Venetian *joie de vivre* animates a scene known to have been painted in antiquity and described by the Roman writer on art, Philostratus the Elder. A river of wine was believed to flow on the island of Andros, and beside it, on the tree-shaded grass, men and women are flirting, playing the lute, dancing and drinking—the first celebration in paint of the lightheaded joy and freedom imparted by wine.

The Venetians liked luxury and pleasure, but they also had a religious side, which appears in the pictures of Titian's contemporary, Jacopo Tintoretto. As retiring as Titian was sociable, Tintoretto worked for the many halls and chapels belonging to the various religious fraternities in which Venetians liked to cluster. He heightened drama with strong diagonals and an intense contrast of light and shade, which, in his deeply felt later work, came to symbolize grace and human nature. Often Tintoretto chose an unusual view of a familiar scene, so lending it freshness and urgency: in "The Presentation of the Virgin" we are at the bottom of a steep flight of steps which dominates the canvas; at the top stands the high priest, while in the foreground her mother Anne indicates to the child Mary the way up the steps. Tintoretto used technique to explore and deepen his central theme and in this respect is truly in the classical tradition implied by the term Renaissance, but he had cleared a way for baroque painters who were to make unusual, even sensational, views an end in themselves.

Beautiful objects and landscape, opulence, spectacle, and the drama

Venetian courtesans and their pets in a luminous painting by Carpaccio.

DIALOGO
di
GALILEO GALILEI LINCEO
AL SER.ᵐᵒ FERD. II. GRAN. DVCA DI
TOSCANA

of human existence—these facets of the new Italian way of life were conveyed so perfectly by Venetian painters that they became a stimulus both to contemporaries and to future generations. Women wished to be as beautiful as Giorgione's Venus, men as strong, poised, and elegant as Titian's "Man with a Glove"; both hoped to enjoy life as much as the revelers in Titian's "Bacchanal," while experiencing also an abundance of God-given grace such as Tintoretto depicted in the glowing, thunderous sky of "Saint Mary the Egyptian." A full and versatile way of life, idealized perhaps but true in the main, was to become one of the driving forces in Europe's social development.

Art of this quality can be produced only in a free society and, as Aretino never tired of repeating, Venice was the one city where "Liberty moves about with banners flying, and nobody to say to her: 'Haul them down!' " When Rome put pressure on universities to limit freedom of learning, the Venetian university at Padua alone continued to grant degrees to Catholic, Protestant, and Jew. A Fleming, Andreas Vesalius, taught anatomy at Padua and there dared to contest the statements of Galen, the Roman authority on medicine whose works had been hallowed by Catholic tradition. Among the Protestants who took a degree at Padua was the Englishman William Harvey, discoverer of the circulation of the blood. Others connected with Padua were Gabriello Fallopio, who gave his name to the Fallopian tubes, and Girolamo Fracastoro of Verona. Fracastoro has a quaint title to fame: he wrote a poem about the venereal disease that had appeared in Italy shortly after the return of Columbus and his sailors from the New World, and it was he who named it syphilis, after the title character of his poem—a Greek shepherd. In the 1520s Fracastoro made astronomical observations with a rudimentary telescope—its first recorded use by a scientist—and he wrote an elaborate treatise reconstructing the homocentric system of Eudoxus, in which the planets rotate in concentric spheres around different axes.

The most famous of the scientists who studied or taught at Padua is Galileo Galilei. He was born in Florence in 1564, the son of Vincenzo Galilei, a musician who helped to pioneer opera. His family background gave young Galileo an interest in the mathematical proportions and harmonies on which music is based, while Platonism, now the Florentine philosophy *par excellence,* taught him to look on the earth,

Aristotle, Ptolemy, and Copernicus are shown on the title page of Galileo's iconoclastic Dialogo, *published in Florence in 1632.*

the planets, the sun, and all the stars as part of one harmonious whole. As an instructor in Pisa, Galileo set himself to reconcile the division—a legacy of Aristotelianism—which was hampering physicists and astronomers: that between the "natural" circular motion of the planets and the "violent" and accidental rectilinear motion assigned to our earthly sphere. In public experiments on the leaning tower, Galileo established that the velocity of falling bodies is independent of their mass or weight, and went on to formulate the principle of inertia, according to which bodies preserve their state of rest or motion indefinitely if not affected by external conditions.

From Pisa Galileo went to Padua, where for eighteen years he taught mathematics. In the glassworks of Venice, the most advanced in Europe, he was able to have a telescope made, and in 1609 he trained it on the sky from the 323-foot campanile of Saint Mark's. This was a momentous night in the progress of mankind. "As I am stricken by an immense astonishment, so I thank God infinitely, who has deigned to make me the only and first observer of an admirable thing which had been hidden to all the past centuries." Galileo had discovered moons revolving round the planet Jupiter, much as the moon revolves round the earth: here was definite visible evidence to support the speculations of Copernicus and others that circular motion round a fixed body is a normal celestial occurrence, and that the solar system can best be explained by the hypothesis that all the planets, including the earth, revolve round the sun.

With a more powerful telescope Galileo next revealed the structure of the moon, sunspots, the anomalies of Saturn, the phases of Venus. He had proved that the so-called immutable heavens were, like the earth, subject to change: he had established the physical unity of the universe and the methodological unity of science. But so ingrained were old beliefs that Cesare Cremonini, one of Galileo's Paduan colleagues, refused to look through the telescope, and in 1616 a Vatican commission censured the Copernican system as contrary to the Bible and heretical.

Galileo gave up his chair at Padua and retired to Tuscany, where Grand Duke Cosimo II afforded him hospitality. There he expounded his discoveries and their implications in *Dialogue on the two chief systems of the world,* the imaginary setting for which is one of the palaces on the Grand Canal. Having examined the book, the Roman Inquisition condemned Galileo for teaching a doctrine contrary to Scripture, namely that the earth is not the center of the world, thus precipitating "disorder and leading souls to damnation." Galileo was cited to Rome and forced under threat of torture to "abjure, curse, and abhor" the opinions he had published. There is probably no truth in the legend that on rising from his knees after the abjuration Galileo muttered the words *"E pur si muove,"* "Nevertheless, it does move." Galileo was obliged to publish his last scientific work, *Dialogues concerning two new sciences,* surreptitiously in Holland, in 1638, pretending that his manuscript had been brought "in some unknown way" to the publishers, Elzevir.

Galileo's discoveries and his condemnation mark the decline of the Renaissance in Italy. First, his successful use of the telescope showed that the future of science lay no longer with the application of knowledge gleaned from Plato, Aristotle, and other classical writers but with specially invented instruments. Secondly, the action of the Roman Inquisition was a categorical denial of the Renaissance spirit of free enquiry. Unfortunately, Galileo's was not the only condemnation. When Giordano Bruno of Naples taught pantheism and a plurality of worlds in an infinite universe, he was burned at the stake by the Roman Inquisition, and another visionary southerner, Tommaso Campanella, paid with twenty-seven years of solitary confinement in political and inquisitorial prisons for his scheme for the moral redemption of mankind in a communistic "City of the Sun." Such police methods marked the end of independent speculation and were soon to cost Italy its intellectual primacy.

Venice could not remain unaffected by the new climate of thought and the government gradually developed an exceedingly elaborate system of censorship. Then, in the early years of the seventeenth century, the Index appeared; within a year it had sharply reduced the activities of Venetian publishing houses which were world-renowned for scholarship and pleasing format. The number of printing presses dropped from 125 to 40.

Political independence was another matter, however, and here Venice continued to resist the encroachments of Rome, supported now by the Spanish troops who occupied so much of Italy. A crisis occurred in

1606, when the Venetian government insisted on a civil trial for two priests suspected of serious crimes. Pope Paul V laid Venice under an interdict, and the Venetian senate called to its aid a Servite monk, Paolo Sarpi, who had made important discoveries in optics and was also a brilliant theologian. Sarpi wrote a complete statement of the claim of the state to conduct its own affairs and to try its own citizens in his *Treatise on the Interdict,* while the clergy obeyed the senate's command to disregard the papal ban. Spain prepared to help the pope by force of arms, but still Venice stood firm, eventually winning the political support of the king of France, who in 1607 arranged a settlement which was generally considered a moral victory for the Venetians. Six months later Sarpi was attacked in the street and wounded by a dagger thrust through the cheek; the would-be assassins fled into safe refuge in the Papal States and it is probable that they were in the pay of Rome. Sarpi recovered and lived to write the famous *History of the Council of Trent,* in which he strongly criticized growing papal autocracy.

In Rome events were moving in a diametrically opposite direction. In 1562, when the composer Palestrina's fame was at its peak, the first emasculated male sopranos—the famous *castrati* of Italian musical tradition—entered the papal choir; these *castrati* symbolized the new mood of the Vatican, where the decrees of the Council of Trent, while improving the moral quality and education of the clergy, sapped all original and creative effort. Michelangelo's "Last Judgment," painted in 1536, is a medieval subject treated no longer with hope but with near despair. While Gregory XIII celebrated the Massacre of Saint Bartholomew with public rejoicing, taxation increased and the population fell. Young John Milton on a visit to Rome ran into trouble with the police for airing his religious views too freely. More and more excellent books were placed on the Index. The Renaissance had yielded to the Counter-Reformation: a tragedy all the more ironical in that Italians had shown no disposition to embrace Luther's doctrines.

As for the other important states during the sixteenth century, Florence revived the republic during the confusion following the sack of Rome, only to see it rooted out forever in 1530 by the imperial armies. The emperor Charles V installed an official despot, Cosimo I, of the Medici family, gave him the title of duke, and married him to his ille-

gitimate daughter. In 1537 Cosimo de' Medici succeeded to the dukedom and for thirty-seven years ruled with wisdom and justice, but his ubiquitous police crushed all opposition. In 1569 Cosimo received from Pius V the title Grand Duke of Tuscany, thus creating a regime which was to last until the extinction of the Medicean line in the eighteenth century. The dukes sponsored useful work digging canals, draining marshes, and improving harbors, but by curtailing freedom of thought and speech they too played their part in extinguishing the Renaissance.

Milan and Naples were both united to Spain, the former ruled by a complex of senate, privy council, and state assembly, the latter by a parliament. Milan was the more prosperous, its craftsmen esteemed for the fine clothes they exported throughout Europe. But in the Castello, ever watchful, stood an alien garrison of Spanish troops, whom the Milanese were obliged to feed, clothe, and pay; the shadow of their cannon darkened the lives of men who knew they were no longer

A sixteenth-century engraving shows gaily dressed Venetian courtiers.

free. In Naples everything was heavily taxed for the benefit of the nobles, so that the philosopher Tommaso Campanella declared that a man had to pay for the privilege of keeping his head on his shoulders. Sicily was particularly unfortunate in suffering the introduction of the Spanish Inquisition, even more severe than the Italian systems. There, as in Naples, trade and industry declined; deforestation, erosion, and malaria ravaged the land and its people.

The economic decline which struck Italy in the second half of the sixteenth and the beginning of the seventeenth centuries extended even to Venice. Just two years after the victory over the Turks at Lepanto in 1571, Venice had to yield her important eastern Mediterranean base of Cyprus to the same enemy. In 1576 a plague claimed fifty thousand Venetian lives, including that of Titian, aged almost ninety, with the result that fewer qualified candidates presented themselves for key positions. In the Rialto, which had once been crowded with Venetian ships, there were now more foreign than native vessels—England, Portugal, Holland, and Spain had wrested from Venice trade in spices, furs, dyes, and silk, in gold, ivory, and slaves. Economic decline sapped morale no less effectively than despotism or foreign rule would have done. Venetians sought to forget in a whirl of revelry and masquerade their vanishing glories: the citadel of commerce began to become the city of carnival.

As Italy lost the Renaissance, the rest of Europe gained it. Francis I might fail to keep Lombardy, but he succeeded in luring Leonardo da Vinci to his royal court at Amboise, where almost daily the king sought him out for the pleasure of his learned conversation. At Francis' palace of Fontainebleau worked Il Rosso of Florence, Francesco Primaticcio of Bologna, and Benvenuto Cellini, who made for the king an exquisite gold saltcellar depicting Earth and Sea. Francis gathered around him humanists reared on the classics which Italians had rescued and translated: notable among them was Guillaume Budé, who built up the royal library—open to all scholars. As a counterpoise to the hidebound Sorbonne, the king endowed the more liberal Collège de France, where Greek was taught, and the courses of which were free to those who could benefit from them.

Farther north Erasmus of Rotterdam, who had studied in Bologna, continued the Italian tradition of textual scholarship: it was he who published the first New Testament printed in Greek, and he found in the Greek author Lucian a model of amusing satire, with which, in his *Praise of Folly*, he was to pillory the foibles of theologians. Even in Spain, the land least touched by the Italian Renaissance, the genius of Tintoretto again caught fire in Toledo under the brush of El Greco, who had been born in Crete a Venetian subject before coming to study in the lagoon city.

But the country which most felt the influence of the Italian Renaissance was England. Sir Philip Sidney was never without his copy of *The Courtier,* a handbook of gentlemanly conduct written by the Mantuan, Baldassare Castiglione. The courtier, according to Castiglione, should be able to read Greek and Latin, play musical instruments, dance, write poetry and, in time of war, fight with bravery, yet always he should preserve a certain nonchalance: perhaps the origin of the English gentleman's famous "amateur" approach and habit of understatement. Shakespeare, though schooled in "small Latin and less Greek," set many of his best plays in ancient Rome and Greece, while his knowledge of Italy, especially of Italian geography, is so detailed that some scholars believe he must have visited the country, as so many of his contemporaries did. English travelers found a special fascination in the villas of Palladio, and soon no gentleman's country house was complete without a pedimented portico, a taste which would spread to the United States during the eighteenth century.

More important even than these visible signs was the transfer which took place to Europe and the New World of the values created from the classical past by the first Florentine humanists, and which now became the basis of the Western educational system. Humaneness, the measured life, public-spiritedness, tolerance, a belief that the world is good and that in it "men can do anything with themselves if they will" —so familiar have these concepts become that we tend to take them for granted, but in fact they were forged, or reforged, by a few gifted and dedicated Italians. It is no exaggeration to say that Italians influenced Europe for good as much through the Renaissance as they had done, fifteen hundred years earlier, through the Roman Empire.

DECADENCE

When Pope Clement VII, in Bologna, in the year 1530, placed the imperial crown on the head of Charles V, Italy once more became part of the Holy Roman Empire. Now grown immense in size, the empire extended from Vienna to Seville, and beyond to the vast Spanish possessions in South America and the East. In this world-empire Italy was no longer, as she had been in the past, the part most advanced in trading skills or wealth. A settlement of the peninsula was made in 1559, when Italy fell by treaty to the Spanish branch of the Hapsburgs. Milan, Naples, Sicily, and Sardinia became Spanish possessions, held down by strong Spanish garrisons, while the rulers of most of the remaining states owed their thrones to Spanish support. Italy, virtually enslaved, fell into decadence. Only in free Venice did the Renaissance linger on until about 1600.

In 1701 the Hapsburgs in Spain died out and were replaced there by French Bourbon rulers. At the convocation for the Peace of Utrecht in 1713 a reshuffle became necessary in which most of Italy, still as part of the empire, exchanged Spanish for Austrian Hapsburg rule. Milan, Naples, and Sardinia came under the direct rule of Austria, and from

The magnificent Gallery of Geographical Maps in the Vatican Museum has a ceiling decorated with frescoes by seventeenth-century artists.

1737, when the last of the Medici dukes died, Tuscany also had an Austrian ruler. The predominance of Austria was to endure until Napoleon invaded Italy in 1796 and reorganized it a couple of years later.

For close on two and a half centuries, then, Italy for the most part was enslaved to foreign rule. It was a period of political darkness, broken here and there by flickers of independence and vigor. Venice, as we have seen, took an independent line in the sixteenth century, and even as late as 1606 was able successfully to defy the alliance of Spain and the papacy on a matter of principle. The other vigorous state was Piedmont. Here a succession of crafty dukes played off the French and Spaniards against each other with such success that Piedmont acquired more and more territory along the southern margin of the Alps, and in 1720 the island of Sardinia; thenceforth the former dukedom of Piedmont came to be called the kingdom of Sardinia. Whereas during the sixteenth and seventeenth centuries other Italians let their swords rust and their muscles grow flabby, the people of this small kingdom developed into a nation of soldiers.

These two hundred and fifty years are characterized by crushing taxation, which left the Italian people wretched and sometimes starving, especially in the kingdom of Naples, where the rule of viceroys reached a high pitch of corruption; by strict censorship, which curtailed original thinking; and by a policy of regionalism, which caused Italians to think largely in local terms. Gone were the days when a Machiavelli could urge all the peoples of Italy to work together for national reconstruction and the common good. In the misery of physical and mental oppression few Italians looked beyond the present or their own restricted horizons.

Spanish rule was much worse for Italy than Austrian rule proved to be, and the 150 years when Spain dominated the peninsula represent the lowest point of Italian fortunes. Spain almost alone of the European nations had escaped the classical revival—the nude for example never became popular with painters—and Spain, with her tradition of intolerance toward Moors and Jews, stood at the opposite pole from Italy, with her humanism and her intellectual curiosity. So that with the entry of Spanish power and Spanish values, all that was best in the Italian Renaissance either dried up or, as we shall see, sought expression in "safe" activities such as music and opera.

The period of Austrian domination brought a slight improvement, in the sense that the Enlightenment was sweeping Europe and found its way even into the reactionary Hapsburg court. From 1748 to 1796 Italy, furthermore, enjoyed peace, during which many of her rulers—imitating Emperor Joseph of Austria—felt safe in introducing reforms. Charles Emmanuel III (r. 1730–1773) did much for the kingdom of Sardinia, where he founded two universities, while Charles IV (r. 1734–1759), with the help of an able minister, the Tuscan Bernardo di Tanucci, took the first steps toward introducing a uniform legal code into the kingdom of Naples, and curtailed some of the clergy's privileges. But the money he gained from the latter reform he spent not on social services that would benefit the very poor but on building Naples' Teatro San Carlo, with six tiers of boxes, and the palace of Capo di Monte; also on excavations at Pompeii and Herculaneum.

Perhaps the most effective of these minor enlightened despots is to be found in Tuscany. That country during the seventeenth century had been misruled by the Medici grand dukes, who owed their thrones to Spanish arms and an army of spies. The dynastic line became steadily more decadent until the last Medici duke, Gian Gastone, was so repulsive, with his thick lips, bloated cheeks, and double chin, that the bride who had been found for him, a Bohemian heiress, refused to cohabit with him, and the line became extinct. Thereupon the Hapsburg emperor appointed his third son, Leopold, to rule the duchy. Grand Duke Leopold I (r. 1765–1790) broke up the big estates, abolished feudal servitude, and made all citizens equal in respect to taxation. He was the first European to abolish torture and the death penalty. He reformed the universities of Pisa and Siena; he even abolished the Inquisition. But all this he did by a series of decrees, without any backing from his people, still after centuries of subjection, sunk in apathy. Moreover, Leopold acted not in the interests of the Tuscans as such but in order to promote efficiency, and because he saw in the Church a threat to his own absolute power. It comes as no surprise to learn that he was a brother of Queen Marie Antoinette.

In the Papal States, likewise, though both centuries were a period of enslavement and intellectual stagnation, a distinction has to be made between the seventeenth century and the eighteenth. In the former a series of martinet popes practiced nepotism and imposed severe taxa-

tion. In the forty years leading up to 1676 the population had declined by a third, while taxes in the same period had doubled. It became extremely difficult, says a Venetian observer, for young men to make a living, and vast numbers, without a vocation, had no recourse but to enter the priesthood.

At the end of the century Pope Innocent XII, by his own example and through a series of reforming measures, rooted out nepotism and paved the way for the respectable popes who characterized the eighteenth century. Their main task was to fight a rearguard action against the European sovereigns now bent on destroying ancient privileges, notably the immunity of clerics from taxation. In this the popes failed, and their failure is epitomized by Clement XIV's bull, *Dominus ac Redemptor,* which in 1773 suppressed the Society of Jesus, traditional champion of papal prerogatives. Since the Jesuits had educated large numbers of upperclass boys, this was to have important social consequences in Italy.

Against so somber a political background Italy as a whole stagnated. Individual Italians here and there succeeded in making a name for themselves, but it is surprising how many, in order to do so, had to go abroad. At the beginning of this period a gifted young Sicilian deacon with a flair for politics emigrated to Paris; as Cardinal Mazarin he became prime minister to Anne of Austria during the childhood of Louis XIV; and by his tact and moderation healed the civil war of the Fronde, which had threatened to split France irretrievably. Cardinal Giulio Alberoni was another who could find no outlet for his political gifts at home; a gardener's son, he moved to Spain, where he became the minister of Philip V and favorite of Elizabeth Farnese. He was the second Italian within a century virtually to rule a foreign country.

The three leading Italian poets of the eighteenth century all sought fortune and freedom abroad. Metastasio of Rome wrote hundreds of melodramas, many of them libretti for operas, and although almost forgotten today, he was hailed by Voltaire as a genius and became the idol of the court when he settled in Vienna. His near-contemporary, the Venetian Carlo Goldoni, wrote everyday comedies with real characters instead of the usual repertoire of types. He infused a breath of fresh life into an exhausted literature, but his audiences preferred escapism and the Inquisitors showed disapproval at his touches of satire. Gol-

A well-attended jousting tournament of the sixteenth century is staged in the piazza before Saint Peter's Basilica in Rome.

doni went off to Paris, where he was to spend the last thirty-two years of his life running the *théâtre italien*. Finally, Vittorio Alfieri, the bold Piedmontese count who wrote republican, antityrannical dramas in a manly style preferred the free air of Paris and London to the bigoted stuffiness of Turin. Two other writers who left Italy not from choice but by decree of the authorities were Lorenzo Da Ponte, banished from Venice to Vienna, where he wrote the libretto of *Don Giovanni* for Mozart—he was eventually to emigrate to the United States—and Pietro Giannone, whose *History of the Kingdom of Naples,* published in 1723, defended secular government against the privileges of the clergy; Giannone paid for his outspokenness with excommunication, a miserable life of exile, and death in prison.

A strict and bigoted censorship was the curse of Italy at this period. The classics were emasculated as they had been in the Middle Ages, and although still the staple of education, they were taken as models of language and style, while their content was ignored. Since a poet was discouraged from expressing his deepest aspirations not only by censorship but by the abject, conforming spirit inherent in political subjection to a foreign power, he tended to write mere trifles, few of which have withstood the test of time. There was almost no philosophical speculation, least of all in the sphere of political theory, no writer daring to challenge the accepted view that political absolutism was an instrument of Divine Providence. It is symptomatic that in the field of history, which had been forged anew by Italians of the Renaissance, the one considerable writer, Gian Battista Vico of Naples, devised a new theory of the nature of history, the underlying principle of which is that man cannot discover truth; all he can know is what his own mind has created. Vico also taught that human development is cyclical: after an era of civilization men will once again behave like wild beasts. In his twofold denial of man's power to mold his own destiny Vico showed himself a creature of Italy's Age of Pessimism.

Most startling of all is the absence of a sense of Italy. None of the Italian rulers, least of all the popes, ever followed an "Italian" policy. What patriotism there was remained local. Not even Alfieri conceived a practical plan for ensuring freedom and independence for the whole of Italy. Any reforms inspired by the Enlightenment were purely administrative and regional; they were never actuated by any heartfelt

King Ferdinand IV of Naples, dressed in the guise of a humble fisherman

cry of freedom for Italy. The explanation is to be found partly in the traditional Italian habit of making the best of things as they are; partly in a complete sense of powerlessness. Apart from a few thousand seasoned campaigners in the kingdom of Sardinia, the only troops in Italy were parade guards and the masked revelers of carnival.

In the fine arts the Renaissance had been the age of the straight line, swordlike, upright, direct; the seventeenth and eighteenth centuries are the age of the curve, twisting, billowing, often cringing. In architecture the greatest single achievement is the Neapolitan Giovanni Bernini's Piazza of Saint Peter's, where 380 colossal columns, surmounted by 162 statues, are disposed in two great sweeping curves. The baroque, though not a style native to Italy, was handled by Italians almost as though they had invented it; and indeed its triviality and escapism were in keeping with their own mood. Countless baroque churches were decorated either with ceilings such as those of the Venetian painter Gianbattista Tiepolo, which seem to soar right up through endless series of saints and angels to the verge of Heaven, or with inlaid colored marbles of prodigious, dizzying complexity, as in the church of Saint Caterina in Palermo.

It was in the comparatively independent atmosphere of Venice that the best painting was done, but even here it is symptomatic that the two foremost artists, Antonio Canale, better known as Canaletto, and Francesco Guardi, chose as their subjects not people but—more safely —views of their city, its canals and gondolas and pageantry. The great Roman engraver, Giambattista Piranesi, depicted prisons, and stern Roman monuments, through which his personages wander like ants. Prisons were an obsessive image with sensitive Italians in this age of Italy's enslavement and reappear in the great book of the humanitarian reformer Cesare Bonesana, *On Crimes and Punishments,* in which he denounced the death penalty and pioneered the idea that imprisonment should be used not as a reprisal but as a deterrent. Bonesana, like so many of Italy's freest spirits, went to live abroad, but his book influenced Leopold of Tuscany and led to reforms there.

Of all the arts the one that flourished most was music. It could not be censored, and it provided a much-needed escape to happier worlds. The most important Italian invention of the period is opera. At the end of the sixteenth century a group of musical amateurs, called "De

Above left: Baroque musical instruments. Below: Carravaggio's "The Concert."
OVERLEAF: *"The Square of Saint Mark's," by Canaletto, a native Venetian*

Bardi" because they met in the house of Giovanni Bardi in Florence, tried to discover how ancient Greek actors had chanted their tragedies. Although they failed in this aim—the secret of Greek music appears irretrievably lost—they did evolve a new kind of musical drama, in which plot, not music, took first place, and as a means of forwarding the plot, invented recitative. Claudio Monteverdi of Mantua wrote the first real opera, *Orfeo,* produced in 1607 in his native town, then moved to Venice, where he wrote many more. Venice can boast the first opera house, opened in 1637, and it was a Florentine, Gianbattista Lulli, who took opera to France, where he became a friend of Louis XIV.

In the eighteenth century opera became the favorite art form of European society. The sincerest works were written outside Italy, but the best virtuosi and the whole musical tradition was Italian: Franz Joseph Haydn, for example, received his musical schooling from Niccolo Porpora of Naples. As for Italian opera, what audiences required, according to one contemporary, was "a crafty texture, surprising incidents, variety of meters, frequence of inventions, shortness of recitatives, abundance of songs, deceptions, entanglements, untying of knots, subtleties, oddities, witticisms, allegories, metaphors, and epigrams." Hundreds of composers toiled to implement this complicated recipe. The famous names are Alessandro Scarlatti, founder of the Neapolitan school of music, and composer of over one hundred operas; Gianbattista Pergolesi, who was the composer of, among other works, the famous *Stabat Mater;* Domenico Cimarosa; and Giovanni Paisiello, whose *Nina* was to be Napoleon's favorite opera. Music and Italians became almost synonymous in the minds of educated Europeans.

Italy had entered a backwater; her once-deep intellectual harbors had silted up, daring voyages of the mind had now been superseded by clever ascents to Heaven, in a papier-mâché chariot, from the stage of an opera house. But even in stagnation Italy was considered the school of Europe, because of her past, and travelers from all over the Continent flocked southward to learn the language in which so much great literature had been written, to admire the ruins of Rome and the palaces of the Renaissance, and to buy paintings.

In the troubled sixteenth century there had been few visitors from England, and from that period dates the phrase "Englishman Italianate, devil incarnate." But in the next two hundred years, the age of the

Engravings by Piranesi include scenes of Rome (top left and bottom), a prison fantasy (top right), and tourists at Pompeii (middle right).

Grand Tour, no travelers to Italy were more numerous or freer with their praise than the British. John Milton traveled to Italy just before England's civil war and learned Italian well enough to write poetry in that language. Later came Edward Gibbon, who amid the ruins of the Forum conceived his *Decline and Fall of the Roman Empire.* The architect Inigo Jones studied the villas and palazzi of Palladio and on his return built numerous country houses in that style for English gentlemen. Dr. Johnson, who never made the journey, confessed that "A man who has not been in Italy is always conscious of an inferiority."

Most of the British went to learn, admire, and collect, but one traveler journeyed south with a different motive. James Boswell went to the island of Corsica in 1765. Since 1300 Corsica had been a possession of Genoa, but recently, led by Pasquale Paoli, the Corsicans had been fighting for their independence. Genoa, a shadow of its former self, had been obliged to call on French troops for help. Boswell's sympathies were all with the Corsicans; he wrote a book describing their manly virtues and undertook a one-man campaign to persuade the British government to help with arms and money so that the Corsicans might regain their freedom. He was the first of many remarkable Englishmen who were to conceive that Italians might yet be free, and to assist them with their pens, with money, or by actually fighting. Unfortunately for the Corsicans, in 1768 Genoa sold Corsica to King Louis XV of France; French troops subdued the island, and that is why, when Napoleon was born in the following year, he was not an Italian, a subject of Genoa, but a Frenchman.

In general, French and German travelers thought less of restoring independence to Italy than of enjoying her ancient past. Montesquieu focused attention on the Roman Republic and held it up as a model to Frenchmen sickened with a decadent and ineffective monarchy, while the German Johann Winckelmann studied classical art not only in Rome but at Pompeii and Herculaneum, where the first important discoveries had been made in 1735. Winckelmann founded scientific archaeology and in his *History of Art in Antiquity* expounded the principles of classical art, thus setting the stage for neoclassicism which shortly began to supersede baroque.

It is from the impressions of foreign travelers that we get our most truthful picture of Italy at this time. There was a marked difference between north and south; between Milan, for example, a prosperous manufacturing center, where silk was produced on 1,384 looms, and Naples, with a backward peasant economy, exporting mainly olive oil, and where 90 per cent of the population were illiterate. No less marked was the gulf between rich and poor. The noble families who made up society comprised only about 2 per cent of the population, but most of the wealth belonged to them. Since the decline of Italy's ports, they were now landowners, not overseas traders. They were not as rich as their English and French counterparts; their palaces, it was noticed, were furnished with pictures and little else. They saved on meals—at receptions all the Venetians offered was chocolate and ice water—and spent heavily on prestige-raising carriages and ornate clothes.

In some parts of Italy one in twenty or thirty of the population was a priest, whereas in France the proportion was one in two hundred. Two important new Orders came into being during the eighteenth century: the Redemptorists of Saint Alfonso de' Liguori, and the Passionists of Saint Paul of the Cross. Religion was everywhere respected, but morals varied greatly from city to city. In Rome four thousand murders were committed in the eleven years of Clement XIII's pontificate, whereas Venetians continued to deserve their reputation for gentleness. "The People of Venice," noted Montesquieu, "are the best in the world: there are no guards at all at the spectacles and no rowdiness is heard; nor does one see any brawling."

One feature peculiar to Italian society at this time was the *cicisbeo,* or *cavaliere servente.* He was a lady's recognized escort. He accompanied her in society and to the theater; he was even allowed to attend her toilet in the morning, while her hair was done or her maids dressed her. But as a rule he did not spend the night with her, and we must discount as exaggerated the reputation Casanova had given the *cicisbeo* for habitual libertinage. The *cicisbeo* was really one expression of a society where men had too little to do and women as yet had too little education to enjoy pursuits more intellectual than mild flirting.

"You already find a marked taste for music in the first towns you come across in Lombardy," observed the French traveler P. J. Grosley. "Everyone plays the violin; even the service in village churches sounds much like a concert. . . . The further you advance into Italy the livelier this taste seems to grow, so that . . . Italy can be compared to a diapason

of which Naples plays the octave." Italian society spent much of their time in their boxes at the opera, where they received their friends, gossiped, gambled, and even ate cooked meals. King Ferdinand IV of Naples used to eat huge plates of spaghetti in his box at the opera, grimacing and making monkey antics the while, as the populace in the cheaper seats below roared approval. The most heated discussions were not about politics—almost a taboo subject in Italy—but about the merits of this or that *castrato* singer. Here and at the theater the intellectual content of the work being performed was ignored. What the audience wanted was amusement, diversion, wit. Joseph Addison complained that he had seen a performance at Bologna of a translation of *El Cid* into which the masques of Italian comedy had been introduced: "It would never have pleased the public if a place had not been found in it for these buffoons."

The best amusement of all came at carnival time. The most spectacular shows were staged in Rome, where there were horse races and parades for which noble families fitted out floats, in which they sometimes rode. In Venice carnival lasted throughout the latter part of winter, and so many masked balls were held that visitors formed the impression that life itself in Venice was a masquerade. In the south, carnival parades tended to crystallize around patron saints. Palermo, for the feast of Santa Rosalia in 1770, devised a float which the English traveler Patrick Brydone reckoned to be 70 feet long by 30 wide and 80 high. It was drawn by 56 mules in double file, mounted by 28 postillions in garments trimmed with gold and silver, ostrich plumes in their hats. The float took the form of a conch with raised prow, while the stern expanded into an oval amphitheater to hold a large orchestra surrounding a rococo arch, which sheltered Rosalia's image.

While Italians were engaged in such harmless amusements as these the French Revolution burst on Europe. The rulers of Italy immediately sought to seal off their subjects from the infection of the new ideas. Their instruments were the Inquisition, prison, and, for books containing the word *freedom,* the bonfire. Repression became tighter than ever before. But it could not hold back the tide of revolution, which was to sweep across the Alps in the shape of a French army led by a man who was to change the whole pattern of Italian life more effectively than any individual before him.

The Italian love of intricately planned gardens dates from classical times. Here a 1749 engraving by Vasi shows a rococo garden and villa.

CHAPTER IX

THE REMAKING
OF ITALY

Three times long ago the French had dramatically invaded Italy. First Pepin had answered the pope's call to drive out the Lombard kings; three centuries later the Normans had swept across the Alps to carve out for themselves a new kingdom in the south; finally, in 1494, King Charles VIII had made his brief descent into Naples and discovered for France the civilization of the Renaissance. But the invader who led this new fourth assault was cut from different cloth; he came of an Italian family and originally bore an Italian name—Napoleone Buonaparte. He had been brought up to speak Italian, and his boyhood hero was the Corsican soldier-statesman Pasquale Paoli. Although a French citizen and a general in the French army, he felt a kinship with Italians and treated them with understanding.

There was a second big difference. Earlier Frenchmen had come as conquerors only. They were concerned to acquire territory or booty. But Napoleon came not chiefly to take but to give. He came (admittedly because this would strengthen France) in order to throw out the Austrians and to give Italy the Rights of Man, which Frenchmen had won for themselves in the Revolution and now wished to extend to all

Although the Cathedral of Milan was begun in 1386, the exterior was not completed until 1813, and only then by order of the emperor Napoleon.

Europe. At least in French eyes this was an attempt at liberation.

Austria and France declared war on each other in 1792; and the king of Sardinia, who, as we have seen, ruled Piedmont, the only Italian state with an efficient army, entered the war on Austria's side. Napoleon, with the directory's backing, conceived the idea of defeating Austria by a gigantic flanking attack, across the Ligurian Alps, through Piedmont, to Milan; then up over the Tyrol to the gates of Vienna. Many derided the tactic as the dream of a madman, but having given proof of his worth by saving the republic from Parisian royalists, Napoleon received command of France's Army of the Alps in spring 1796. He was then aged twenty-six. With fewer than fifty thousand half-starved soldiers, in tattered uniforms, many without boots and obliged to march with straw tied round their feet, Napoleon divided the Piedmontese from the Austrians. He defeated the former, made peace with the king of Sardinia, then swept into the Po valley, where in a series of brilliant victories he defeated the Austrian armies. Carrying the war into Austrian territory in April, he obtained from the archduke Austria's renunciation of her claims to Lombardy in trade for France's recognition of Austria's interests in Venice. One thousand years of Venetian independence was thus extinguished.

Meanwhile, Napoleon also found time to harass the pope, cause of particular displeasure to the French directory. Napoleon was instructed to march south and depose Pius VI, who, like every European ruler, had denounced France's new republican regime. Napoleon did march south but for once failed to obey orders. Steeped in Italian history, he realized that without a pope the cities of the Papal States would fragment into warring factions. This would make central Italy liable to be swallowed up by Naples, then ruled by an even more determined enemy of France than the pope, Maria Carolina. Instead of deposing the pope, Napoleon merely weakened him by seizing forty million francs in gold and three of the northern provinces of the Papal States.

He then began to organize the territory he had freed: roughly the whole of northern Italy save Venice. There was much doubt in Paris as to what should be done with the liberated territories. Should they, like Holland, be turned into a sister republic, modeled on France and bound to her by alliance? Or were the Italians so sunk in decadence as to be unworthy of "the reign of virtue," as republican government was euphemistically described? The directors called for reports, and the majority recommended that the Italians should merely be treated as pawns to secure favorable terms with Austria.

Napoleon however took a different view. Able to talk to Italians in their own language, he used what little time he could spare from campaigning to evolve a plan for the political reorganization of the region. He even discussed the problem of Italy's future with Italian scholars, such as the physiologist Lazzaro Spallanzani, and the translator of Homer, Melchiorre Cesarotti, as well as with members of the small middle class of Milan: lawyers, notaries, and the like. He found them well read in Montesquieu and Rousseau, and much better prepared than the directors believed to try the experiment of self-government. Napoleon therefore urged Paris to give him a free hand in organizing northern Italy as a republic, and because he had been so successful in everything else, the directors agreed.

In the summer of 1797 Napoleon drafted the constitution and the laws of the new Cisalpine Republic, as northern Italy was now termed. The executive was to consist of five directors, the legislature of two councils, Napoleon himself appointing the first directors and council members, though it was laid down that future members would be elected by the Italians themselves. The republic extended from the Piedmontese frontier to the Mincio River, and from the Alps to the borders of Parma, Tuscany, and the Papal States. Green being Milan's traditional civil color, Napoleon gave the new republic a flag reminiscent of the tricolor: red, white, and green. It was the first time for many years that Italians had had an emblem they could call their own, and two generations later this red, white, and green flag was to be adopted as the banner of a new united Italy.

In the region of Genoa, where the oligarchy had collapsed, Napoleon founded a second state modeled on similar lines: the Ligurian Republic. To both he preached the importance of self-reliance based on a renewal of martial qualities, and he enrolled regiments of Italian volunteers to fight side by side with French troops against the Austrians. At the same time he made clear that the cost of their liberation and of the occupying troops must be met by the Italians. This was a burden that Italians resented even more than the transfer to Paris, under the terms of various treaties, of many of their best works of art and famous manuscripts such as the *Notebooks* of Leonardo da Vinci.

In 1798 Napoleon sailed to conquer Egypt, and almost at once the directory, grown inept and weak, through a series of stupid moves undid the work achieved by their statesmanlike general. By the end of 1799 the French had had to evacuate all Italy save Genoa, and the Austrians were back as rulers.

Napoleon became First Consul, or head of state, in October, 1799, and within eight months was again in Italy. By the victory of Marengo, snatched from the jaws of near defeat, he won back Piedmont, Liguria, and Lombardy, and in 1802 reorganized the Cisalpine Republic, with a modified constitution and himself as president. But this arrangement did not last long. Hired assassins in the pay of foreign governments repeatedly tried to kill Napoleon, and he, believing himself to be the embodiment of the French Revolution, wished to ensure the continuity of all he stood for, even should he fall to an assassin's bullet. Napoleon therefore established a hereditary empire, modeled to some extent on Charlemagne's, and in December, 1804, crowned himself Emperor at Notre Dame, in the presence of the pope. It followed that the Cisalpine Republic must be transformed into a kingdom within the empire. This was done in 1805. Napoleon tried to persuade his brother Joseph to accept the crown of this new kingdom. Joseph, however, who wished to be given the higher status of Napoleon's heir, declined the crown. Napoleon decided to take it himself. In 1805 he placed on his own head the Iron Crown of the Lombards and, with his stepson Eugène de Beauharnais as viceroy, began a long series of public works throughout northern Italy, including better schools and the completion of the cathedral of Milan, in which the coronation ceremony had been held. At the same time the Ligurian Republic was annexed to France.

Napoleon signed a treaty of neutrality with the king of Naples in October, 1805, but only a month later the rabidly anti-French Queen Maria Carolina persuaded her husband to break it by admitting British and Russian troops. It was not the first time the queen had infringed a promise of neutrality, and Napoleon resolved "to hurl this criminal woman from her throne." As a French army closed in, she sailed for Palermo, and Joseph Bonaparte accepted the crown of Naples.

The kingdom of Naples was the most backward country in western Europe. Half the land belonged to the Church, the other half to 2 per

A victorious Napoleon leads his troops against the Austrians at Marengo.

cent of the population. The overwhelming majority of the people, it was said, did not own enough land to be buried in. Peasants lived like serfs, some obliged even to pay a tax on water; on one estate in Luciana, two hundred were herded into a single barn every night to sleep like cattle on straw. Joseph and his efficient advisers, who looked upon themselves as missionaries of republicanism, ended this iniquitous situation. They abolished the feudal rights of the barons. They requisitioned Church property and divided it among the poor. They pensioned off all but two hundred of the monks—retaining these few to look after Monte Cassino—and limited the number of future priests. They paid off a crushing national debt and reformed taxation. They introduced the newly codified French law system which bore Napoleon's name, to replace eleven unwieldy systems of law, the legacy of Romans, Byzantines, Normans, Angevins, Aragonese, and others. It was one of the most efficient salvage operations in history. When Joseph became king of Spain in 1808, he was succeeded in Naples by Napoleon's brother-in-law, Joachim Murat, who continued reforms that soon brought prosperity to a traditionally poor land.

Napoleon meanwhile, locked in his struggle with England, was obliged to impose an embargo on all enemy ships entering Continental ports. For the success of his scheme it became imperative to control the whole Italian coast: in 1807 he annexed Tuscany, in 1808 Rome and the Papal States. The following year he declared Rome a free imperial city and the pope's temporal power at an end. The popes had now come to believe that their temporal sovereignty was an integral part of their papal prerogatives; Pius VII therefore excommunicated Napoleon, and he, believing that Pius had no right to use spiritual weapons in defense of his temporal power, bundled the pope off to a closely guarded exile in Savona.

Tuscany Napoleon made an integral part of the French Empire and entrusted its rule to the most intelligent of his sisters, Elisa. She developed industry, founded a girls' school, got the Carrara quarries working again after decades of inactivity, and established a school for promising young sculptors. As her brother, whom she adored, signed decrees and letters with a big capital N, Elisa took to signing *her* decrees with a big capital E. Once, however, when she countermanded an order by a French minister, Napoleon reversed her decision and reminded her severely that she was merely an administrator of technically French departments, and could not overrule decisions from Paris. It is often said that Napoleon carved up Italy merely to gratify members of his family, but this is not so. His brother and sister had little real power; they were essentially administrators of a republican system—and Napoleon saw to it that they did their job properly.

The Italian Republic lasted only fifteen years; French rule in Naples six years, in Tuscany seven, in Rome six. When Napoleon fell, the kings and dukes returned with their courts. But something had happened in those few years that could never be wholly checked or reversed. The Italians had tasted political freedom and equality; they had even glimpsed national unity. As Napoleon said in a message on New Year's Day, 1797: "Italy unfortunately has been long excluded from the number of the European powers. If the Italians of today are worthy of resuming their rights, some day they will see their country appear with glory among the powers of the earth." This was a true prophecy. But, Napoleon had insisted, the Italians must prove themselves worthy. They must become men, fighters for freedom. Tens of thousands of Italians, volunteers and conscripts, had fought in the Grande Armée, their uniforms embroidered with the slogan "All free men are brothers." Many had fallen on the parched plateaus of Spain and in the snows of Russia, but many others had returned, and were to act as a leaven on the soft dough of their long abject fellows. The great lesson of the Napoleonic era in Italy was this: all men are born free, and if they find themselves in chains it is up to them to fight to the death to throw off their servitude.

The Congress of Vienna decided the future of Europe after the fall of Napoleon. There in 1815 the reactionary chancellor of Austria, Prince Klemens Metternich, defined the term "Italy" as "merely a geographical expression," and for the next thirty years he was to try to prevent the term having any other meaning. As the result of the Congress of Vienna Italy, with eighteen million inhabitants, was fragmented into seven states: Lombardy-Venetia, which was an Austrian province; Tuscany; Parma with Piacenza; Modena with the smaller duchies of Massa-Carrara and Lucca—all ruled by members of the Austrian royal house; the kingdom of the Two Sicilies, ruled by a Spanish Bourbon; the kingdom of Piedmont-Sardinia; and the Papal

OVERLEAF: *Meeting in Lyons, a delegation of leaders from the Cisalpine Republic proclaim Napoleon (seated on dais) as their president.*

States. Only the last two were ruled by native Italians. All the republics had been abolished. Feudal rights were restored, and in Rome for example the Index and the Inquisition were reintroduced.

Some Italians refused to accept this outrage to their incipient liberties, and in 1820 there began the first attempts to throw off foreign rule. They were organized by secret societies, whose members were chiefly ex-officers and men of the middle class. The most famous of the secret societies, the Carbonari, took its name, symbolically, from *carbone*—coal—black in color, but which on being kindled burns with a bright flame. These first risings were never a "popular" movement; they were local, with no clear aim in view other than to strike at the foreigner.

The poet Lord Byron helped the Carbonari of Romagna personally as well as with money and arms, but the Austrians swooped before they could strike an effective blow, and Byron, disappointed, sailed instead to help set Greece free. At each court the Austrian minister had numerous private spies and political agents, so it was not difficult for Metternich to track down the patriots. In Lombardy a distinguished playwright named Silvio Pellico joined the Carbonari. He was caught and sentenced to fifteen years' imprisonment in the fortress of Spielberg, in Moravia. On his release Pellico published a moving account of his years in prison, which did more than any other book to arouse national indignation. Nearly all the patriots who took part in a series of risings between 1820 and 1831 were jailed or exiled, but their example helped keep awake the national consciousness.

The leading patriot-conspirator was Giuseppe Mazzini. He was born in Genoa in 1805, the son of a professor of medicine. After studying law he joined the Carbonari, was betrayed by a police spy, spent six months in prison without trial, and then withdrew to Marseilles. Thenceforth he was to lead the life of an exile and to act as the brains and conscience of future insurrectionary movements. Mazzini was an impressive-looking man, with a lean face, strong straight nose, prominent brow, and flashing dark eyes. His expression was stern, and he usually wore a black velvet suit. He was a deeply earnest man, with an unshakable belief in the popular will, in republicanism, and in the need for social justice.

Mazzini believed that recent risings had failed because the secret societies did not know precisely what they were working for and be-

cause they relied too heavily on the intervention of France, now, under
Louis Philippe, the rival of Austria. What was needed, Mazzini believed, was a deep and widespread movement of spiritual renewal, religious and moral in character; and to meet this need in 1831 Mazzini founded a society at Marseilles called Young Italy. He defined Young Italy as "the brotherhood of Italians believing in a law of Progress and Duty, who being convinced that Italy is called upon to become a nation, hold that she can make herself such by her own efforts . . . that the secret of power resides in unity and constant effort, consecrate thought and action, joined to the great purpose of making Italy a nation of free and equal citizens."

Mazzini organized Young Italy as a society, headed by a central council, which met outside Italy, and in touch with provincial offices in Italy. Each member had to pay a minimum subscription of fifty centimes a month, and to equip himself with a dagger, a rifle, and fifty cartridges. Except in special cases, no one over forty was admitted. An idealist himself, Mazzini intended to build on the idealism of youth. By 1833 Young Italy had sixty thousand members.

Mazzini began to organize uprisings in various parts of Italy. All of them, however, proved failures. It would have been difficult even for a trained soldier to initiate guerrilla warfare at a distance, and Mazzini was less adept with the dagger than with the pen. Mazzini's really important work was to keep the idea of a united Italy alive in his periodical, *Giovine Italia,* in articles, in "open letters" to influential men, and in a vast correspondence with members of his organization and with potential supporters throughout Europe.

Within Italy patriotism was kept alive by books, plays, and opera. There was a revival of interest in great Italians of the past, especially Dante, and Cesare Balbo wrote the *History of Italy under the Barbarians* inspired throughout by the ideal of national independence. Before his imprisonment Silvio Pellico wrote the patriotic tragedy *Francesca da Rimini,* in which Francesca, put to death by her husband for loving Paolo the Fair, movingly symbolizes Italy in love with Freedom. Among the operas which became popular because of their patriotic allusions were Rossini's *William Tell,* and Verdi's *I Lombardi,* followed a year later by *Ernani.*

Of the books proposing a practical solution to the problem of foreign rule, the most influential was *The Moral and Civil Primacy of the Italians,* by Vincenzo Gioberti, a liberal Turin priest living in exile in Brussels, where his book was published in 1843. Gioberti argued that Italy had been greatest in the eleventh century, when strong popes had kept the empire at bay; now Italy must make herself independent by forming a confederation of her princes with the pope at their head. The existing systems in the different states were to remain intact. The moral lead was to come from the Catholic Church, as in Belgium, where Catholic sentiment was associated with the national movement. Whereas Mazzini believed that Italy could be freed only by revolution, Gioberti advocated a solution of Italy's problems by peaceful reforms. His book was to be the Bible of the moderates.

In 1846 the reactionary Gregory XVI died and the new pope, Pius IX, was known to be more liberal. He removed the main restrictions on freedom of the press within the Papal States and allowed the Ro-

Giuseppe Mazzini (right), founder of the organization Young Italy, and one of his early converts, Giuseppe Garibaldi (left), leader of the Redshirts

mans to form a civic guard, a traditional sign of trust in the people,
since the guards were armed. At once the pope was hailed as the
savior of Italy foreseen by Gioberti, and even Mazzini saluted him in
an "open letter." But in fact Pius was far less liberal than patriots
believed, nor could a pope ever be brought to lead a purely national
movement aimed against another Catholic nation.

The pope's measures were imitated elsewhere in Italy: the grand
duke of Tuscany also agreed to the formation of a civil guard, and
King Charles Albert of Piedmont allowed three newspapers to be
started. By far the most important of these newspapers was *Il Risorgimento,* the Resurrection, edited by Count Camillo Cavour. In its pages
was begun a crusade for independence, reform, and a league of Italian
rulers against Austria. The journal's name caught people's imagination
and was eventually to be applied to the whole independence movement.

Since 1834 there had been a lull in political action, but this was

*King Victor Emmanuel II (left) and Camillo Cavour (right), whose news-
paper* Il Risorgimento *gave its name to the movement for Italian unification*

dramatically broken in 1848 as the result of two revolutions abroad. In February the French deposed King Louis Philippe and proclaimed a republic; in March the Viennese people rose against their government, Metternich fled, and the emperor agreed to give Austria its first constitution. The tide of events seemed to have turned in Italy's favor, and the Milanese, who suffered most from Austrian rule, were the first Italians to rise, on March 18. In the glorious Five Days a poorly armed people succeeded in driving out Marshal Radetzky and fourteen thousand Austrian troops. Venice, led by Daniele Manin, a brave lawyer of Jewish descent, also threw out its Austrian garrison. Both cities looked to the army of Piedmont, the only trained Italian soldiers, to hurry east and inflict a decisive defeat on Radetzky.

Charles Albert of Piedmont was a sad, pale Hamletlike figure known as Re Tentenna (King Shilly-Shally). He dreaded republicanism, and although he would have liked an independent Italy, he was of two minds about going to help the republicans of Milan and Venice. He lost four vital days wavering, and when he finally marched the Austrian army had dug in to strong positions. In this, their first war of independence, the Piedmontese gained some initial advantages, but during the summer the Austrians, who had received reinforcements, heavily defeated Charles Albert at Custoza. On August 6 the Austrians reentered Milan, while the Piedmontese army scurried home. Another bid to beat the Austrians the following spring was defeated in a week. Charles Albert in shame abdicated in favor of his twenty-nine-year-old son, Victor Emmanuel II, and slunk off to die in Portugal.

In 1848 almost all Italy had been up in arms, but by spring 1849 the only states holding out against Austria with any chance of success were Venice and the republic which had been founded in Rome. (The people of that city had risen after Pius IX disappointed all Italian patriots by refusing to throw in his lot with the national cause. The pope had withdrawn to Naples, where he appealed to Catholic nations to send troops to end the republic and restore him to his throne.) Mazzini had arrived in Rome to take the lead in government, and the defense was entrusted to Giuseppe Garibaldi, a Piedmontese fisherman's son who had gained valuable experience in guerrilla warfare during a long exile in South America.

Garibaldi had five thousand ill-trained and poorly armed troops, but

their morale was high, and he himself, with his handsome face and
golden beard, wearing a white South American poncho and a black
ostrich plume, infected them with his own courage. On April 30, 1849,
they defeated ten thousand French troops sent to help the pope by
Louis Napoleon, president of the new French Republic. In July the
French returned to the attack, this time with odds in their favor of three
to one. Rome had to capitulate, but Garibaldi with three thousand
volunteers slipped out intending to march northeast to aid the last
remaining bastion of freedom: Venice. Once again the defense was
led by Daniele Manin, but the assault proved too much for his patriots.
Cholera and typhus swept the lagoon city, while the Austrians, for the
first time in history, dropped bombs from balloons. Thousands in
Venice died, and finally food became so scarce that on August 24
Manin was obliged to capitulate. Garibaldi tried to reach the doomed
city by fishing boat but was overtaken by Austrians. He managed to
reach shore and struggled on, famished and almost exhausted, until
his wife Anita collapsed and died in his arms. Garibaldi eventually
escaped to America, while Manin went to live in exile in Paris. Over
Venice, and in a sense over all Italy, the flag of Austria again flew. But
although no one could be sure of it at the time the seed of a united Italy
had been sown in the blood of these patriot-martyrs.

One good result of the liberal tide of feeling which swept Europe
in 1848 was that the king of Piedmont had granted his subjects a constitution, and unlike other Italian constitutions, it was not torn up in
the reaction of 1849. As it was later to become the basic law of all Italy
for almost a century, it is worth considering here. The constitution
provided for two-chamber government, a senate that was nominated
by the king and a chamber of deputies that was elected, these bodies
sharing their legislative power with the king. The executive consisted
of responsible ministers. Catholicism was the official religion, but the
press was free.

This constitution opened a political career to ordinary citizens for
the first time. Formerly, only rulers—mainly foreigners—or their ap-
pointees could govern, but now it was open to any man, if sufficiently
gifted, to play his part not only in ruling Piedmont but in working for
national unity. Here in the north, Italian patriotism had a secure home
base, and for the next eleven years leaders of the independence move-

ment began to hope for expansion outward from Piedmont rather than in terms of sporadic scattered rebellion.

Very soon Count Camillo Cavour, editor of *Il Risorgimento,* came to the fore in Piedmont. His family were noble and his first job had been as page to King Charles Albert. He served as an officer in the Engineers but resigned at twenty-one to farm the family estates. Using new agricultural machinery from abroad, he made a big success of farming. Then he traveled, chiefly in France and England, taking notes on all the good things he saw, from parliamentary government to railways and banks. At forty he entered the government and two years later, in 1852, became prime minister.

In appearance Cavour was unprepossessing: potbellied, with short, stumpy legs, a blotched face, gray eyes almost invisible behind thick, steel-rimmed spectacles, hands habitually stuck into the pockets of his crumpled gray trousers. His speaking voice was monotonous in tone. But behind this vague and unelectrifying exterior was a sharp, clear mind, courage, and the charm necessary in a diplomat.

Cavour came to power with two deep beliefs. First, Piedmont should be built up into a prosperous industrialized modern state; it should have good roads and railways, factories and banks. Secondly, Piedmont could never overthrow Austria alone, and therefore must work with some powerful ally. The obvious choice was France, where Louis Napoleon had just seized power and was about to revive the empire.

Cavour and Mazzini did not like each other. Cavour was a practical politician prepared to work slowly and at times unscrupulously toward a limited goal; Mazzini was an all-or-nothing idealist. Cavour was a monarchist, Mazzini a republican. Mazzini wanted Italian unity, but Cavour at this time considered it still a remote dream. They agreed on one thing, however: that the pope should play no part in future events. Gioberti, who had once proposed the pope as leader, in 1851 published *The Civil Renovation of Italy,* in which he urged not the pope but King Victor Emmanuel to lead Italians into their promised land. Cavour would not have gone as far as Gioberti; all he wanted at this stage was to create a kingdom of Upper Italy.

In 1854 France and Britain went to war with Russia over the Crimea. Cavour, as part of his plan for proving that Piedmont was a power to be reckoned with and for gaining the friendship of Napoleon III, as

During the heroic "Five Days," March 18–22, 1848, the people of Milan set up barricades such as this and fought in the streets to repulse the Austrians.

Louis Napoleon was now known, sent a contingent of Piedmontese troops to fight beside the French and British. The Piedmontese put up a good show, giving Cavour a right to speak in the Peace Congress.

Cavour's friendship with Napoleon III steadily ripened, and in 1858 the two men met at the health spa of Plombières in the Vosges. There the French emperor promised an army to help the Piedmontese drive the Austrians across the Alps and to make a kingdom of Upper Italy. In exchange Piedmont would give France Nice and Savoy.

Cavour returned to Piedmont and began to mobilize a strong army. A National Society had recently been formed under the watchwords "Italy and Victor Emmanuel" to encourage volunteers and to raise money for rifles; Garibaldi, back from America, had joined it, and Manin, in Paris, had given it his blessing. Now it brought five thousand men from various parts of Italy into the Piedmontese army. In April, 1859, as Cavour had hoped, Austria presented an ultimatum at Turin, demanding disarmament within three days. Cavour disregarded the ultimatum, whereupon Austria declared war, and Cavour invoked his new alliance with France.

Rome's Café Greco, a gathering place for the literary and political elite.

Though he had never commanded an army before, Napoleon III placed himself at the head of the 120,000 French and 60,000 Piedmontese. On June 4 the French alone won a battle at the silk-town of Magenta. On the twenty-fourth the French and Piedmontese together won a much bloodier victory at Solferino. Forty thousand were killed or wounded, and many of the survivors succumbed to typhus. A Swiss stretcher-bearer, Jean Henri Dunant, was so appalled by the suffering and inadequate medical facilities that a few years later he founded the International Red Cross.

Napoleon too was appalled by the loss of life. The Austrians had retreated but were still in Italy, in strong positions; it would take months, and the loss of many more French lives, to oust them. But what disturbed Napoleon even more was that Tuscany and Emilia had risen and were demanding annexation to Piedmont. Napoleon had foreseen a free kingdom of Upper Italy as one of four equal-sized Italian states loosely grouped in a federation with himself as a kind of protector; he had no wish to take part in the creation of a large state of north and central Italy, which might soon grow to include the whole peninsula—not a godchild but a rival. Without telling the Piedmontese, Napoleon went to meet the Austrian emperor at Villafranca and there, as Italians thought, he betrayed Italy by signing peace.

Villafranca came as a bitter blow to Cavour. France, he felt, had let him down, since the hated Austrians were still in Venezia. He resigned, but was to return to power in 1860. Yet Piedmont had gained much from the war: Lombardy, Tuscany, and Emilia. Nice and Savoy were duly ceded to France, and Garibaldi, who had been born in Nice, never forgave Cavour for sacrificing his home town.

With Villafranca ended the second act of the Risorgimento drama. Cavour had extended the power of Piedmont but failed to push as far as the Adriatic. The Austrians were still dominant in Italy. Now the third act was about to begin, in which Mazzini's pen, Cavour's brain, and Garibaldi's sword were all to combine in a final effort.

Both wars of independence had failed because they had been fought in the north, where the Austrian army was based and could be quickly reinforced. With hindsight it seems obvious to us that the better way of freeing Italy must be from the south northward, rather than from the north southward. It was Mazzini, in exile in London, who realized

this, and it was Mazzini's idea that an insurrection should be fomented in Sicily, as the result of which Garibaldi would land and free the island from Bourbon troops.

In 1859 one of Mazzini's closest friends, Francesco Crispi, a forty-year-old Sicilian lawyer, traveled to Sicily in disguise. He found conditions ripe for rebellion. The new king, Francis II, was almost an idiot, a tool of the Austrians and the pope. Students, noblemen, peasants, were all eager to throw off a corrupt and oppressive regime. Walls were chalked with the slogan "Viva Verdi!"—not a eulogy of the composer, as the police thought, but a political call, meaning "Viva V(ittorio) E(manuele) R(e) D'I(talia)." The rebellion was planned for the following spring, and on March 2 Mazzini sent the Sicilians his blessing: "What are you waiting for? Dare, and you will be followed. But dare in the name of national unity."

The first spark of rebellion was struck in the workshop of a Palermo plumber, Francesco Riso, near La Gancia monastery, on April 4, 1860. Riso and thirteen workmen fought the Bourbon troops, counting on simultaneous rising by Palermo noblemen, which, however, failed to take place. Riso's men were all killed or executed. But other minor rebellions broke out in various towns, and the spirit of resistance was kept alive by hopes that Garibaldi would soon be coming.

As soon as he heard of the Palermo insurrection, Garibaldi hurried to King Victor Emmanuel and asked for a contingent of Piedmontese troops. The king, on Cavour's advice, refused, for such an act would have offended Napoleon, whose friendship was still vital to Piedmont. Garibaldi then decided to go it alone with the volunteers who had already begun to assemble near Genoa. Altogether the volunteers numbered 1,089; about half were professional men, including a hundred doctors, the rest workers. On the night of May 5 the Thousand, as the freedom fighters were styled, embarked on two antiquated steamers, the *Lombardo* and the *Piemonte*. The *Lombardo*'s engine would not start, and finally she had to be given a tow-start by her sister ship. Some obsolete guns and muskets were loaded in Tuscany, but ammunition was short. On May 11 the ships arrived off Marsala, in western Sicily, a thousand men against a Neapolitan garrison twenty-five times that number. It seemed a hopeless undertaking, and Cavour, who had opposed the expedition, was quite certain it would fail.

A stalwart pasta merchant drying some noodles surveys the passing scene.

The *Lombardo* ran aground at the entrance to Marsala harbor, but Garibaldi succeeded in getting his men safely ashore, despite fire from Neapolitan warships. The accidental presence of two ships of the English navy made many think that Garibaldi had an agreement with the British government. This was not so, though Britain, sympathetic to Italian unity, did help behind the scenes. By her naval presence she dissuaded Napoleon, who since the battle for Rome hated Garibaldi, from sending the French navy to cut off the Thousand once they landed.

The first battle took place four days later at Calatafimi, where two thousand Bourbon troops were dug in on a steep hill near the town. Helped by young Sicilians who had rallied to them, Garibaldi's Thousand, wearing red shirts as a sort of uniform, attacked with bayonets and routed the Neapolitans. Calatafimi was a notable victory, not only because it proved the fighting qualities of Garibaldi's irregulars, but because it fired the Sicilians, who now thronged to join the Redshirts. When Garibaldi arrived in Palermo, hundreds of Sicilians had already risen, thus demoralizing the Neapolitan garrison of twenty thousand. Garibaldi quickly entered the city, where the people helped him by building barricades and cutting the royal troops' communications with Naples. On June 6 the Bourbon general Giovanni Lanza signed an armistice, evacuated the city, and agreed to evacuate the whole island.

Garibaldi had assumed the dictatorship of Sicily in the name of Italy and Victor Emmanuel. Cavour wished him to annex the island to Piedmont immediately, but Garibaldi and his right-hand man, Crispi, preferred to delay. If Sicily were at once annexed, they argued, then Cavour would close the southern campaign. Cavour was not yet thinking of the unification of Italy, but Garibaldi was, and he determined to free Naples, then march on Rome and Venice. The situation was further complicated by the many Sicilians who wanted their island to become an autonomous state. For the moment a decision was postponed while Garibaldi, his army strengthened by recruits enrolled from all over Italy by the National Society, proceeded to clear the northeastern corner of the island. This he achieved by his victory on the promontory of Milazzo on June 20. It was a costly battle, for he lost more than seven hundred dead and wounded, but it brought all Sicily, save the citadel of Messina, into his power and made it possible to invade the mainland.

Victor Emmanuel, a romantic young man with a pretty mistress and a taste for military adventure, had a great personal liking for Garibaldi and had secretly given him his blessing when he sailed for Sicily. But he understood from Cavour the danger that would arise if Garibaldi, who had strong republican sympathies, repeated in southern Italy his success in Sicily: "If Garibaldi can pass to the mainland and take possession of Naples," wrote Cavour, "he becomes the absolute master of the situation. . . . King Victor Emmanuel loses almost all his prestige; in the eyes of the great majority of Italians he is no more than Garibaldi's friend." On Cavour's advice, the king sent Garibaldi a letter ordering him to halt at the Strait of Messina.

Aware of the king's liking for him and, even more, of the need in war to seize the favorable moment, Garibaldi disregarded the letter. On August 18–19 Garibaldi crossed the Strait. Naples' young king Francis II had already panicked and in one period of twenty-four hours telegraphed five times for the pope's blessing. He withdrew north across the Volturno River, allowing Garibaldi on September 7 to enter Naples. Garibaldi was now dictator of Sicily and dictator of Naples. He began to make plans for a march on Rome.

Cavour was faced with an extremely difficult situation. Garibaldi's success had convinced Cavour that the unification of Italy was a possibility. But dividing northern and southern Italy like a long wall were the Papal States. If Garibaldi's conquests were to be linked physically to the kingdom of Piedmont, it must be at the expense of part or all of the Papal States. Garibaldi was bent on attacking Rome and ending the pope's temporal power. France was bound by treaty to uphold that power, so an attack by Garibaldi would either be repulsed by the strong French army defending Rome or, if successful, put Cavour in the dilemma of disowning Garibaldi in order to retain France's friendship, or of recognizing Garibaldi and facing a war with France which would probably undo the triumphs of 1860.

Cavour found a typically brilliant compromise. He decided to occupy only the papal provinces of Umbria and the Marches, leaving the pope in possession of Rome and the territory immediately around it, known as the "patrimony of Saint Peter." The temporal power would thus be respected, but "the boot of Italy would be stitched." Cavour obtained France's consent to this plan, and although it meant risking war with Austria, on September 18 the Piedmontese army crossed the

frontier into the Marches. Papal troops put up only mild resistance, the key town of Ancona fell, and Victor Emmanuel rode south to take command of his army. Francis II's troops made a last-minute attempt to recapture Naples but were decisively defeated by Garibaldi on October 1–2 at the battle of the Volturno. On October 26, near the Volturno, Garibaldi met Victor Emmanuel and welcomed him with words that have become famous: "I salute the first king of Italy!"

Garibaldi asked to be given full powers in the Two Sicilies for a year, but Cavour had already decided on the annexation, by means of a plebiscite, of all the newly occupied territories. Garibaldi, whose popularity had become dangerous, was told that his services would no longer be required. To a friend, Admiral Carlo Persano, Garibaldi confided: "This is what happens, Persano, they just treat men like oranges, pressing out the juice to the last drop, and throwing the peel away." In November he returned to his lonely home on the island of Caprera, between Corsica and Sardinia.

Sicily, Naples, Umbria, and the Marches all voted overwhelmingly to form an integral part of an Italy "one and indivisible" under King Victor Emmanuel, and before the year 1860 was out Italy was no longer merely a geographical expression but a united nation. True, the pope still ruled in Rome and the Austrians in Venetia, but the incorporation of these two territories into Italy would not be long delayed. Unification had been largely achieved by the efforts of Mazzini, Cavour, and Garibaldi. The mass of the eighteen million people in Italy had played no part in the movement for unity: they had been too long crushed by misrule to storm ramparts en masse. But it has been well said that although the unification of Italy was never a popular movement, it was carried out in the people's interests by men who believed in their cause. Mazzini is the man most responsible for this. He was deeply disappointed that his united Italy should emerge as a monarchy, and he continued to live as before chiefly in exile, but it was Mazzini's sense of history that gave the popular stamp to the movement. "*Young Italy*," he had written almost thirty years before, "is Republican and Unitarian. It is republican because all true sovereignty resides essentially in the nation, the sole progressive and continuous interpreter of the supreme moral law . . . and because our Italian tradition is essentially republican."

Looking for a chance to start a new life, many Italians like this young man immigrated to America in the late nineteenth century.

CHAPTER X

MODERN ITALY

Italy was made; it remained to make Italians. Ever since the decline of the Roman Empire, patriotism had been local, and a man's proudest boast was that he was a Perugian, a Florentine, a Neapolitan, a Sicilian. It would take time before a silk weaver in Milan could feel himself a fellow citizen with an olive grower in Calabria, the more so since there was a sharp difference in living standards between the comparatively prosperous north and the impoverished south. Roads and railways, conceived on a regional basis, now had to be extended to the whole nation. Schools had to be built to give children the education essential to parliamentary democracy, and scholars had to devise a new history course which would relate Italy's past to the culminating event of unification. Whole industries had to be created if Italians were to catch up with the high standards of living in other western European countries. And all this had to be done with scant natural resources. Italy had little coal and iron; and not until very recently were petroleum and natural gas discovered. Equally important, she had no tradition of democratic government, no trade unions, almost no experience in the responsibilities of a free press. She had no traditional

Italy's inventiveness in modern design is typified by Pier Luigi Nervi's dramatic Stadio Flamino, using the new structural technique of prestressed concrete.

foreign policy, no long-standing friends; and on the banners of her small army there was no stirring roll call of national victories. It is a wonder that Italy survived at all, and it was in a crucible of suffering and self-doubt that the first generation of "Italians" came to be forged.

In the Middle Ages Italy for long had been dominated by the powerful German emperors beyond the Alps, and from the years 1860 to 1945 the one continuously important influence on the young Italian people was first the growth, then the aggressive strength, of a strong German nation. During this period many of the ideas and much of the sufferings experienced in Italy had their origin in Germany.

The first results of the rise of Bismarck's Prussia proved beneficial to Italy, by making it possible to round off Italian frontiers. In 1866 Bismarck declared war on Austria, and Italy came in on Prussia's side. In return for her support she received Venezia. In 1870 France went to war with Prussia and was obliged to withdraw the French garrison protecting the pope in Rome. This was a long-awaited moment, and Victor Emmanuel's Italian army immediately marched on Rome, entering the city on September 20, a date commemorated in the street names of many Italian cities and towns. Rome and the patrimony of Saint Peter voted by plebiscite to become part of Italy, and the pope's temporal sovereignty was limited to the Vatican, the church of Saint John Lateran, and the summer residence of Castel Gandolfo. The pope refused to accept the loss of his temporal power and angrily shut himself in the Vatican, firing a Parthian shot in the form of a stern injunction that no Italian Catholic should take part in his country's government, either as voter or deputy. This was to hamper seriously the working of democracy until its repeal by Pius X.

In Rome, now the new capital, a succession of short-lived governments went slowly ahead with the work of modernizing and strengthening Italy. Abroad, they entered the game of power politics. Piqued at France's seizure of Tunisia, which Italy regarded as her sphere of influence, she threw in her lot with Germany and Austria-Hungary by concluding, in 1882, the Triple Alliance.

From Germany too in the form of the works of Karl Marx came a strong movement of revolutionary Socialism; the economic feudalism in the south, rigged elections, and the growing failure of party government were the chief objects of its attack. Bombs were thrown and

in Naples an attempt made to assassinate the king. It was generally felt that a firm hand was needed, and in 1887 Francesco Crispi became prime minister. This Sicilian, a man of extremes, had prepared the way for Garibaldi's invasion of Sicily, and now, aged seventy-eight, was a warm admirer of Bismarck's ironhanded methods.

Crispi immediately cracked down on the newly formed Italian Socialist Party. When rioting broke out in Sicily, Crispi sent in troops, proclaimed a state of siege, and set up military tribunals which punished the ringleaders with sentences generally considered much too heavy. As protest marches and other disorders continued, Crispi dissolved Socialist societies and workers' associations throughout Italy. This was an unwise move, because there were real grievances: for example, many workers were living below the subsistence line and had no legal right to strike. The Socialist movement went underground.

Abroad Crispi was disturbed that Italy lagged so far behind France and Britain as a colonial power. He conceived a typically theatrical

A native Ethiopian painting depicts the Battle of Aduwa, March 1, 1896.
OVERLEAF: *The painting "The Fourth Estate" shows strikers of 1905.*

plan for founding an empire in Africa. At first he was successful, conquering Eritrea and Somaliland on the Red Sea. In 1890 he declared Ethiopia an Italian protectorate. But the conquest of that mountainous country proved slow and arduous. In 1896, determined to end the campaign, Crispi imprudently ordered an all-out attack. At Aduwa, General Oreste Baratieri's army was cut to pieces: more than ten thousand Italians fell or were captured. The shock to public opinion was such that Crispi had to resign and he retired from public life. His periods of office had been disastrous in themselves and had set a dangerous example of dictatorial ascendancy. Moreover, the Socialist movement flared up again in 1898 with more riots and bomb-throwing, reaching its pitch two years later with the assassination of King Humbert.

With the new century the left-center Liberals came to power and gave the country fifteen years of parliamentary government. The guiding force, even in the short periods when he did not hold office, was Giovanni Giolitti, a career civil servant with a flair for economics. Giolitti granted the workers full liberty to strike and brought in measures for public health, inexpensive housing, insurance against industrial accidents and sickness, as well as regulating the working conditions of women and children. But the means whereby he controlled parliament were ominous for the future. Party system had completely broken down, and it was Giolitti who manipulated parliament, rewarding those who voted for him with high appointments.

Gradually, Italians worked their way toward prosperity. At last they had found a source of industrial power in hydroelectricity, which gave an impetus to engineering firms such as FIAT and soon made it possible for the silk and cotton industries to increase greatly their number of looms. A high birth rate and a lack of economic opportunity had resulted in wide-scale emigration, especially to the United States; and in the years just before World War I the millions of lire sent back home by these migrants was of major importance in erasing the trade deficit. The budgets from 1898 to 1914 showed a healthy surplus. Even colonial adventures abroad proved prosperous, and the former Turkish colony of Tripoli was seized in 1912–13 and renamed Libya.

In the summer of 1914 Germany and Austria plunged Europe into war. By the terms of the Triple Alliance Italy was not bound to help her allies in an offensive war, and Giolitti, now out of office, recommended to his successor that Italy remain neutral. This was certainly the wisest course for a young and in many ways immature nation. But there were many Italians who wished to see Italy imitate ancient Rome, to win not only military glory but also the so-called Italia Irredenta, a defensible Alpine frontier extending to the Brenner Pass, Trieste, and Dalmatia, which for centuries had formed part of the Venetian Republic. Austria refused to cede these territories in exchange for Italy's intervention on the side of the aggressors, but Britain and her allies (the Triple-Entente) promised that they would cede them to Italy in the event of victory. A secret pact embodying these terms was signed in April, 1915, and is known as the Treaty of London. On May 23 Italy entered the war on the side of the Allies.

The Italian war effort was concentrated against the Austrians along the very unfavorable military frontier inherited from 1866. Although the Italians had an advantage in numbers, the Austrians were dug in on the southern slopes of the Alps. The Italians could achieve no military gains along the central ramparts of the Alps, and they could not afford to leave them undefended, a situation which was costly in terms of troop deployment. What offensive the Italians did launch was on the eastern flank where they hoped to gain the Adriatic port of Trieste. A dozen disastrous assaults were tried, morale slipped dangerously, and the Germans, who had not previously engaged the Italians, came to the Austrians' aid. In October, 1917, their combined forces launched an offensive on the Isonzo River at Caporetto, broke the Italian Second Army, and sent 400,000 Italians fleeing westward to the Piave River. There the retreat was halted and the Italian line stiffened by five British and five French divisions. In October and November, 1918, as the Austro-Hungarian Empire crumbled, the Italians on this front made a spectacular advance and regained all their lost territory, as well as the South Tirol, formerly held by Austria. On November 3, 1918, Austria wearily signed an armistice.

At the Versailles Peace Talks new states had to be created in order to fill the vacuum caused by the disappearance of the Austro-Hungarian Empire. One of these states was the kingdom of the Serbs, Croats, and Slovenes (later officially Yugoslavia), which Woodrow Wilson insisted would be viable only if it included Dalmatia, with its long Adriatic coastline. Italy got the South Tirol, but Italians were angry

and disappointed that they did not also get Dalmatia, promised to them by the Treaty of London. To offset the loss of Dalmatia a flamboyant poet-airman, Gabriele d'Annunzio, at the head of black-shirted volunteers, occupied the disrupted Slavic city of Fiume (Rieka) on the Adriatic coast and successfully held it for more than a year. In November, 1920, by virtue of a treaty between Italy and Yugoslavia, Fiume became a free city, and in January, 1924, the signatories redefined it as Italian. But Fiume was poor compensation for the lost Dalmatia.

At home also the postwar years were a period of disappointment and uncertainty. Unemployment, strikes, and inflation paved the way for Communist action. In September of 1920 workers seized engineering factories and attempted to run them themselves, for their own profit. Giolitti, who had returned to office, played the situation coolly, refrained from sending in troops, and was rewarded by seeing the complete failure of the workers' experiment. But so much disorder was bound to bring a reaction. It was not long in appearing.

Benito Mussolini was born in 1883, the son of a Romagna blacksmith of strong Socialist views. After training to become a schoolteacher, young Mussolini entered politics as a Socialist, and became editor of the leading Socialist newspaper, *Avanti*. He fought in the World War, attaining the rank of corporal and was wounded. In March, 1919, he founded at Milan a club of some 150 young men, mainly ex-soldiers, calling it a *Fascio di Combattimenti*. Taking the name of workers' groups which had existed in cities all over Italy, *Fascio* was an allusion to the rods and axes carried by the lictors in ancient Rome, and symbolized the strong, united Italy which Mussolini hoped to see emerge from the prevalent social unrest. Mussolini's brand of *Fasci* sprang up all over Italy. At first they were nationalist and socialist, but soon Mussolini found it more advantageous to enlist the support of big business, and directed his Fascists to fight the Socialists. Wearing black shirts and organized in squadrons —hence their name, Squadristi—Mussolini's men used gangster methods to break strikes and to blow up Socialist headquarters. They were looked upon by many as Italy's only hope against the Bolsheviks.

In 1921 Mussolini and 34 other Fascists were elected to parliament. At this time there were about 152,000 enrolled Fascists, of whom only a third were working class. Their aims as defined by Mussolini were

The serenity of Capri remains unchanged throughout Italy's turbulent history.

restoration of the authority of the state, social reform, national prestige abroad, and at home a planned economy. The following summer the Socialists called a general strike. The Fascist Blackshirts broke the strike, seizing socialist leaders, destroying their offices, smashing their presses, and taking over essential services, then used disorder as a pretext for seizing key administrative buildings. In October, 1922, they converged on Rome. The government was powerless, and on October 29 Victor Emmanuel II asked Mussolini to form a government. Fascism had arrived and was to dominate Italy for twenty-three years.

The autocratic behavior of Crispi and Giolitti had long since brought parliament into disrepute and prepared the way for continuous rule by a strong man. Mussolini's ideas were more German than Italian: he had adopted Nietzsche's aggressive individualism and Hegel's theory that the state is more important than its members, but he preached these doctrines with a flamboyant oratory that was typically Italian. Mussolini possessed a remarkable gift for whipping up emotion in a large crowd. By 1925 he had acquired sufficient power to outlaw all opposition, end the freedom of the press, and construct a Fascist State. Totalitarian in character, it was to be ruled by himself, now known as Il Duce, the Leader, assisted by a grand council of eighty members, most of whom he personally appointed.

Mussolini had risen to power because he promised a frightened people the end of strikes and of industrial anarchy. This promise at least he kept. But he achieved social peace only at the cost of absorbing all industry within what he called the Corporate State and severely limiting civil rights. He obliged employers and workers alike to join government-controlled Fascist Syndicates, whose role it was to draw up collective labor contracts binding on both sides. Strikes and lockouts were prohibited, and disputes settled by special labor courts. Tight government surveillance coupled with national pride produced a modicum of efficiency where free enterprise had failed, and despite a very high birth rate (which Mussolini encouraged with an eye to building his army) the country became almost self-supporting in food.

Although not a religious man, Mussolini saw in the Catholic Church an ally in his struggle against anarchy and Communism. In 1926 he began secret talks with the Vatican in the hope of gaining papal recognition of the Italian state: since 1870 the popes had declined to admit

Above: Mussolini reviewing his North Africa troops. Below: Il Duce *amongst a group of followers during the "March on Rome," October 24, 1922.*

the existence of a state that had stripped them of their temporal possessions. These talks proved successful, and in 1929 an agreement was signed whereby the Vatican recognized the kingdom of Italy, while Mussolini for his part agreed to a number of Church demands, among them that religion should be taught in state schools and that the state should recognize Church marriages as legally binding. Though the Church received large sums in state bonds, in reality it paid a high price for the Lateran Pact, since the Fascists acted on their maxim that the state must be all-powerful and prevented any clerical criticism of the regime being reported in the press. Many had the impression that the Church wholly condoned a dictatorial system of government.

The *fasces,* which Mussolini had chosen as his emblem, were a deliberate reference to the great days of ancient Rome, and Mussolini was constantly reminding his countrymen that they were heirs to their ancestors' empire. Mussolini was also a close student of *The Prince,* in which Machiavelli of Florence had urged a strong ruler to regenerate Italians by, so to speak, a course of muscle-building and the inculcation of martial virtues. Mussolini wrote a thesis on *The Prince* in 1924 and cast himself for the role of a modern prince, a tough, unscrupulous military conqueror. For ten years he kept the peace, while building up Italy at home, but it was obvious to observers abroad that Mussolini's own increasingly swashbuckling manner and the whole concept of a government devoted to national pride must eventually end in an aggressive war. The victim Mussolini chose was Ethiopia, for the disaster of Aduwa forty years before still rankled.

Mussolini declared war on Ethiopia in 1935. Both Italy and Ethiopia were members of the League of Nations, and that body forcibly denounced the war. Fifty-one nations voted to impose economic sanctions, although the two products which might have thwarted Italy's attack—oil and coal—were exempted from the sanctions. Mussolini caused a scare by threatening to leave the League; France, already fearful of Germany's growing power, hesitated to risk losing Italy's friendship, while Britain, her navy much reduced by international agreements, feared a military showdown in the Mediterranean with Italy. France's foreign minister, Pierre Laval, was particularly adroit and unscrupulous in delaying effective sanctions by the League.

No European people had a better colonial record than the Italians.

Of all the Western nations they had shed least blood in acquiring overseas territories and displayed most tolerance to colonial peoples. But now that record was hideously besmirched as Italian airplanes bombed civilians and Italian soldiers unleashed poison gas on a helpless people. The League's halfhearted sanctions never really bit deep on Italy, and served only to nettle the Italians. In May, 1936, Mussolini publicly announced to a thunderous crowd the fall of Ethiopia.

The Ethiopian war was not only an indefensible act of aggression, it had terrible consequences for Italy. Mussolini had incurred the detestation of all liberal-minded people in Britain, France, and the United States; moreover, he resented the League's criticism of his behavior, so that there remained for him only one possible ally in Europe, that other leader of a totalitarian state, Adolf Hitler. Most disastrous of all, the cheap victory had convinced Mussolini that he was a great man of war, and the Italians great warriors. Thenceforth Mussolini was to envisage military force as a sure means of attaining his goals.

In 1936 the Spanish civil war broke out between right-wing Nationalists and the left-wing Loyalists in government. Under the pretext of saving a Catholic country from Bolshevism, and strongly supported by the Church, Mussolini sent almost a hundred thousand Italian volunteers to fight for the Nationalists, the largest contingent of foreign troops and an important factor in Franco's eventual victory. Since Hitler also actively supported the Nationalists, the Spanish war drew the Führer and Duce still closer together. When Hitler invaded and annexed Austria in 1938, Mussolini, far from resisting this threat to Italy's northern frontier, invited the Führer to Rome. In the autumn of that year, Mussolini aped Hitler by issuing anti-Semitic laws: Jewish aliens who had settled in Italy since the war were to be expelled, while Italian Jews lost some of their political and civil rights.

Mussolini was eager to emulate Hitler's coup in Austria by some gain in the Balkans. For many years Italy had been building up her economic interests in the backward mountain-kingdom of Albania, across the Adriatic Sea. In April, 1939, Mussolini picked a quarrel with Albania's King Zog, landed troops, and quickly occupied the country. Albania was poor in resources and to Italy more a liability than an asset. But it helped enhance the fiction of a great new Italian Empire. Then in September, 1939, Hitler invaded Poland; for the second time all

Europe was at war and Italy faced a choice of participation or neutrality.

Mussolini had no deep personal liking for Hitler. Fascism might have its bullies but it was never a deeply irrational and violent movement like Naziism, and there is a touch of fear in Mussolini's description of Hitler as a "madman." Nevertheless, there were two strong forces driving Italy into the war even after Mussolini's declaration of nonbelligerency in 1939. These were the cult of military glory which Mussolini had done so much to foster and, as in 1915, greed for new territory. After Hitler's successful Blitzkrieg of 1940 in the north, which resulted in the conquest of Denmark, Norway, Holland, and Belgium, Mussolini resolved that he could no longer sit idly by; Italy must share in the spoils. As the Germans approached Paris, Mussolini declared war, an act which Churchill called "a stab in the back."

Where once the Roman legions had gained spectacular victories, in Greece and in North Africa, Mussolini's mechanized armies suffered humiliating defeat. Tens of thousands of Italians were captured and spent the war in the prison camps of England; an ironic sequel, for England had been Italy's best friend in her struggle for independence. Italy became completely dependent on German raw materials and on German *panzer* divisions, which occupied the whole peninsula.

The loss of North Africa made possible an Anglo-American landing in Sicily on July 10, 1943. Fifteen days later opposition in the Fascist grand council compelled Mussolini to resign as dictator. While jubilant crowds shouted "Down with Fascism!" and removed party emblems, a new government was formed by Pietro Badoglio. On September 8, Badoglio surrendered unconditionally to the Allies.

Hitler, however, still occupied northern and central Italy, and in a coup which reads like an adventure novel German parachutists snatched Mussolini from imprisonment on a mountaintop in the Abruzzi and brought him to Hitler in Munich. There the Führer commanded the Duce to continue leading the Italian people in their joint struggle against the Allies, and Mussolini, never more the German's puppet than now, abjectly agreed.

Italy is a land easily defended with modern weapons. Dug in on the steep hills, German heavy artillery held up the Allied advance through the winter of 1943 and the spring of 1944. Rome did not fall until June 4, 1944. Not until the spring of 1945, when the front in Germany had already cracked, did the Allies succeed in capturing key northern cities: Ferrara, Verona, Genoa. Mussolini, joined by his mistress Clara Petacci, made frantic efforts to escape to Switzerland, before being caught by partisans and shot. The bodies of the Duce and his mistress were taken to Milan and, strung up by the legs, exposed to the abuse of angry crowds. A few days later the war in Europe was over.

Fascism had proved a disaster for Italy, but, in retrospect, it can be seen as pragmatically useful, however evil. Since 1945 dozens of states throughout the world have achieved independence and been handed the supposedly foolproof system of parliamentary democracy which a few countries of western Europe had taken many painful centuries to evolve. The vast majority of these new states have failed to make democracy work and have fallen to dictators. Only when the injustice and megalomania of dictatorship have been experienced at first hand and found to be even more painful than the muddle of a young democracy can a new state be said to have attained political maturity.

The tragedy of Mussolini may be regarded also as a catharsis. When he fell, certain ugly humors were purged from the Italian body politic. His ignominious and degrading demise stands, and is likely to stand for a long time to come, as a warning of what happens to a man who puts force before justice, national honor before international understanding, and his own will before the will of a freely elected parliament. Certain it is that since the fall of Mussolini Italy's parliamentary system has worked better than ever before, and the country has enjoyed not only just government but unprecedented prosperity.

To understand the new development in Italian politics since 1945 it is necessary to go back to the beginnings of united Italy. In 1870, when Rome was taken from him, the pope forbade Italians to vote or stand for office. That meant that in Italy, the most Catholic country in Europe, the government could never be in any real sense Catholic, though it is true, of course, that many Italians besides the unbelievers disregarded the pope's injunction. The injunction persisted until 1905, when Pius X reluctantly allowed Catholics to vote and enter the Chamber of Deputies, believing this to be the only means of damming a tide of Socialism. Ten years later the Catholic Popular Party, or *popolari*, entered the political arena. Created by a brilliant, broadminded Sicilian priest, Don Luigi Sturzo, it was not a secular arm of the Roman Church

OVERLEAF: *Past and present life styles contrast in contemporary Naples.*

but a party guided by Christian principles able to appeal to all voters on the merits of its political platform. In 1919 the party won 100 seats, coming second only to the Socialists. In 1922 the Popular Party was invited to form a government, but could produce no suitable leader, Sturzo, as a priest, being barred from sitting in parliament. With the rise of Fascism, the *popolari* offered the one possible central rallying point against the Blackshirts, but the Vatican was displeased with Sturzo's autonomous line, and when the choice came Pius XI opted to collaborate with the Fascists rather than back the Popular Party in a proposed coalition with the Socialists. In 1924 Sturzo had to emigrate, and in 1926 the Popular Party was shut down by the Fascists.

It re-emerged in 1943 as the Christian Democratic Party, headed by an austere political journalist of humble birth from the Trentino, Alcide de Gasperi. He had a fine record of resistance to Fascism and, like Sturzo, was a broad-minded but fervent Catholic. He insisted that the Christian Democrats must be free from clerical control and pursue a policy of moderate reform in alliance with other democratic parties. In June, 1946, Italy voted to become a republic, and the following year received a new constitution embodying two-chamber government. In the first elections the Christian Democrats obtained a clear majority, and de Gasperi formed a government. Until his death in 1954 de Gasperi helped steer Italy through a dangerous period, with the Communists threatening to seize power by force. Even after his death the Christian Democrats continued to be the most important party.

Italy is now living in a changed world, where domestic political issues are dwarfed by the larger struggle between the West, the U.S.S.R., and China. The Christian Democrats are firm believers in friendship with the democratic West, and a majority of Italians support this policy, partly because of close family links with the United States, to which Italy has given so many millions of migrants. After the Russians forcibly suppressed the 1956 insurrection in Hungary, Italian Communists have ceased to regard the Soviet Union as a Promised Land and have concentrated on the social ills at home.

In the economic field, Italy has made a few notable strides. At last natural resources have been found: natural gas in the Po valley; oil in the Abruzzi and Sicily. The south has been opened up by a motorway, and its huge estates divided among smallholders. Sicily, long an agricultural area of extreme poverty, has been given large credits for industrialization and social welfare. Nevertheless, heavy deficits in national finance are usual; strikes have been eroding the spectacular increase in productivity which Italians achieved in the 1950s; and a profusion of political parties makes it difficult to form a government and even more difficult for such a government to survive long.

In the arts Italians have continued to produce excellent work, much of it in the cinema. Immediately after World War II came some memorable neorealist movies, such as Roberto Rossellini's *Open City* and Vittorio De Sica's *Bicycle Thief*. Federico Fellini achieved brilliant social commentary with *La Dolce Vita,* which denounced Rome's idle rich, while Luchino Visconti successfully transferred to the screen Giuseppe di Lampedusa's novel *The Leopard,* a social history of Sicily at the time of Garibaldi. Michelangelo Antonioni has succeeded in reclaiming for art the so-called lost world of the modern industrial city: his *Red Desert* is as significant for modern cinema as Michelangelo's study of the muscular nude was for painting.

In 1957 Italy became a member of the European Economic Community. This increased her prosperity: northern Europe became a market for a variety of products ranging from sweet wines to FIAT cars and Olivetti typewriters, while the unemployed labor force of the south migrated across the Alps to work in German industries.

By joining the Common Market Italy took a major step in becoming part of a larger whole, a new United Europe. This is certainly the most important event since independence in 1860. It reduces the chance of another of those catastrophic European wars which have inflicted such suffering on the Italian people. But more than that: it promises that within a framework of peace Italy will be able to contribute all that is best in her native and acquired skills for the benefit of Europe as a whole. During Italy's most creative period, the Renaissance, each city-state followed its own particular bent or genius, thereby contributing to a wide spectrum of achievement. If Italians can continue to make parliamentary democracy work, it may well be that they are entering another great period of their history, during which, in the arts and sciences, in philosophy and politics, they will make their own inimitable contribution to the building of a Europe richer, freer, more variegated, and more progressive than the empire that emerged from Rome.

CHRONOLOGY

c. 1000–700 B.C.	Etruscans land on shores of Tuscany and build towns
977–443	Greek colonies established in Sicily and southern Italy
753	Legendary foundation of Rome by Romulus
509–c. 500	Romans throw off Etruscan rule; Rome becomes a republic
c. 451	Twelve Tables, first written code of Roman law
390	Rome sacked by Gauls; first of many invasions from the north
343–264	Rome gains ascendancy in Italy
264–146	Punic Wars; Rome extends conquests abroad
107–86	Consulships of Marius, creator of professional army
49	Caesar crosses Rubicon, occupies Rome, and is made dictator
44	Caesar, undisputed master of Roman world, is assassinated
27	Octavian founds principate and takes name Augustus; his reign inaugurates *pax Romana* of Roman Empire
A.D. 98–180	Trajan initiated Golden Century of peace; empire reaches its greatest extent
312–313	Constantine defeats Maxentius at Milvian Bridge; issues Edict of Milan granting formal toleration of Christianity
330	Constantine shifts seat of empire to Constantinople
376–476	Invasions by Visigoths, Huns, Vandals, and Ostrogoths
476	Odoacer, Ostrogoth general, deposes Emperor Romulus Augustulus and assumes new title, King of Italy, bringing about so-called fall of the Western Roman Empire
c. 529	Benedict founds Monte Cassino, first monastery in the West
535–553	Justinian's army invades Italy, drives last of Goths beyond the Alps, brings all Italy within rule of Eastern emperor
568	Lombards invade Italy, peninsula divided into Lombard state ruled from Pavia and Byzantine province centered at Ravenna
755	Donation of Pepin; king of the Franks cedes to pope lands in central Italy that later become core of Papal State
800	Charlemagne, having subdued Lombards in Italy, is crowned Emperor of the West by Pope Leo III in Saint Peter's, Rome
827	Moslems capture Sicily; they begin to harass southern Italy
c. 1000–1300	Rise of maritime republics (Amalfi, Pisa, Genoa, Venice) and rise of city-states (Florence, Milan, Ferrara, Siena)
c. 1030–1090	Normans oust Saracens, conquer Sicily and southern Italy
1265–1321	Dante Alighieri, author of *The Divine Comedy*
1309–1378	Babylonian capitivity; papacy moves from Rome to Avignon
1397	Medici banking network is founded in Florence
1469–1492	Lorenzo de' Medici leads Florence; peak of Renaissance
1494	Charles VIII of France invades Italy; drives Medici from

	Florence, inaugurating a new period of foreign invasions
1494–1498	Savonarola rules Florence, which he reorganizes as oligarchy
1503–1513	Julius II pope; Rome is now center of the Renaissance
1520	Pope Leo X excommunicates Martin Luther
1527	Rome sacked by troops of Holy Roman Emperor Charles V; Venice becomes center of artistic activity
1542	Pope Paul III establishes Roman Inquisition
1559	Treaty of Cateau-Cambrésis affirms Spanish control of Italy
1701–1714	War of Spanish Succession ends Spanish domination in Italy; Austria becomes main foreign power on peninsula
1796	Napoleon invades Italy; brings ideals of French Revolution
1797	Venice, one of many republics formed by Napoleon, is ceded to Austria, ending millennium of Venetian independence
1815	Congress of Vienna; Austria once again dominates Italy
1820–1831	Abortive uprisings against Austria; secret patriotic societies such as Carbonari are formed in Italy
1831	Mazzini launches *Young Italy*; organizes revolutionary cadres
1847	Cavour founds *Il Risorgimento,* a journal whose name he later applies to whole Italian unification movement
1848–1849	Further revolts against Austria put down after initial success
1848	Charles Albert, king of Piedmont, grants constitution
1854	Cavour, prime minister of Piedmont since 1852, sends Piedmontese army to fight for French and British in Crimea
1859	French and Piedmontese defeat Austrians at Solferino; Austria cedes Lombardy, Tuscany, and Emilia to Piedmont
1860	With the "Thousand," Garibaldi takes Sicily and Naples; Piedmontese army takes Umbria and the Marches, leaving Rome to the pope and Venezia to the Austrians
1861	Victor Emmanuel II of Piedmont proclaimed King of Italy
1866	Austria cedes Venezia to Italy
1870	Italian troops take Rome, virtually completing unification
1882	Italy in Triple Alliance with Germany and Austria-Hungary
1915	Italy enters World War I on side of Allies
1918–1922	Italy seized by economic crises; rise of Fascism
1922	King Victor Emmanuel III asks Mussolini to form government
1929	Lateran Pact; Vatican recognizes kingdom of Italy
1935–1936	Conquest of Ethiopia despite sanctions by League of Nations
1936–1939	Mussolini gives military aid to Franco in Spanish civil war
1940	Italy joins Germany in World War II
1943	Allies land in Sicily; Mussolini resigns; his successor declares war on Germany; emergence of Christian Democrats
1945	Italy liberated by Allies; Mussolini killed by partisans
1946	Italians vote to abolish monarchy; nation becomes republic
1957	Italy joins Common Market
1972	Neo-Fascists gain power in parliamentary elections

CREDITS AND INDEX

Page numbers in **boldface type** refer to illustrations.
Page references to map entries are in *italic type*.

A

ABRUZZI, 212, 216
ADDISON, JOSEPH, 171
ADUWA, 201, 204, 210
AISTULF, 81, 84
ALARIC, 66, 71–72
ALBERONI, GIULIO, 159
ALBERTI, LEON BATTISTA, 110, 121
ALBERT THE GREAT, 98
ALBIZZI, RINALDO DEGLI, 113
ALBOIN, 80
ALBORNOZ, CARDINAL, 105
ALEXANDER VI, pope, 127, 129–30, 133
ALFIERI, VITTORIO, 160
ALPS, *2*, *7*, 22, **28**
AMMIANUS MARCELLINUS, 65–66
ANNE OF AUSTRIA, 159
ANTONIONI, MICHELANGELO, 217

APENNINES, *2*, *8*, *87*
APOLLONIUS OF TYANA, 52
ARCHITECTURE, 63, 65, 69, 113, 121, 124, 131, 142–43, 163, 199
ARETINO, PIETRO, 142–43
ARISTOTLE, 98, 134, 146, 148–49
ART, 120, 124, 131, 143–47, 163, 168
ASSISI, *2*, 97–98
ATAULFUS, 72
ATHENS, 14, 48, 49, 110
ATTILA, 72, 133
AUGUSTINE, SAINT, 49, 72
AUGUSTUS, 30–40, 45, 69, 80
AURELIAN, 55
AUSTRIA, *2*, 155–57, 174–76, 177, 179, 182–83, 186, **188**, 189–91, 195, 200, 204–205

AVIGNON, 102–104

B

BABYLONIAN CAPTIVITY, 102, 105
"BACCHANAL," 145, 147
BADOGLIO, PIETRO, 212
BALBO, CESARE, 183
"BANQUET IN THE HOUSE OF LEVI," 143–45
BARATIERI, ORESTE, 204
BARBARIANS, 14, 33, 52, 61, 71–85; fibula, **75**
BARDI, GIOVANNI, 166
BEAUHARNAIS, EUGÈNE DE, 176
BELISARIUS, 77
BEMBO, PIETRO, 133, 145
BENEDICT, SAINT, 74–77
BERNINI, GIOVANNI, 163; interior of Saint Peter's, **128**
"BIRTH OF VENUS," 120

BISMARCK, OTTO VON, 200–201
BOETHIUS, 73–74, **76**, 110
BOLOGNA, 2, 98, 130
BONAPARTE, ELISA, 178
BONAPARTE, JOSEPH, 176–78
BONESANA, CESARE, 163
BORGIA, CESARE, 129, **132**
BOSWELL, JAMES, 168
BOTTICELLI, SANDRO, 119–20, 125; painting by, **118–19**
BRAMANTE, 131
BRITAIN, 45, 47, 58–59
BRUNELLESCHI, FILIPPO, 113; cathedral dome by, **106**
BRUNO, GIORDANO, 149
BRUTUS, LUCIUS JUNIUS, 18
BRYDONE, PATRICK, 171
BUDÉ, GUILLAUME, 152
BYRON, LORD, 182

C CAESAR, JULIUS, 32, 36–40, 42, 66, 110
CALATAFIMI, 194
CALIGULA, 40, 45
CAMBRAI, TREATY OF, 138
CAMPANELLA, TOMMASO, 149, 152
CANALETTO, ANTONIO, 163; painting by, **164–65**
CANNAE, 22, 23
CAPRI, **206**
CARACALLA, 47, 51–52, 68
CARPACCIO, VITTORE, paintings by, **136–37**, 144
CARRAVAGGIO, painting by, **162**
CARTHAGE, 18–23, 27, 72
CASANOVA, GIOVANNI, 169
CASTIGLIONE, BALDASSARE, 153
CAVOUR, CAMILLO, 185, **185**, 189, 191, 193–97
CELLINI, BENVENUTO, 135, 152
CERVETERI: sarcophagus, **11**; tomb, **13**
CESAROTTI, MELCHIORRE, 175
CHARLEMAGNE, 84, 176
CHARLES IV, of Naples, 157
CHARLES V, Holy Roman Emperor, 135, 138, 150, 155
CHARLES VIII, of France, 125, 173
CHARLES ALBERT, of Sardinia, 185, 186, 189
CHARLES EMMANUEL III, of Savoy, 157
CHARLES MARTEL, 84
CHARLES OF VALOIS, 101
CHRISTIANITY, 43, 58–61, 65, 72–77, 80, 95–98, 110, 116–21, 133–34, 138
CHURCHILL, WINSTON, 212
CICERO, MARCUS TULLIUS, 29, 32, 109–12, 127, 143

CIMAROSA, DOMENICO, 166
CINNA, LUCIUS CORNELIUS, 33
CISALPINE REPUBLIC, 175, 176, **180–81**
City of God, The, 72
Civil Renovation of Italy, The, 189
CLAUDIUS I, 40, 45
CLEMENT VII, pope, 135, 138, 155
CLEMENT XIII, pope, 169
CLEMENT XIV, pope, 159
COLUMBUS, CHRISTOPHER, 121, 147
COMMODUS, 50–51, 54
COMMUNISM, 207, 208, 216
"CONCERT, THE," 162
Consolation of Philosophy, The, 74, 77, 110
CONSTANCE, COUNCIL OF, 104–105
CONSTANTINE, antipope, 81
CONSTANTINE I, 58–61, 63, 64, 65, 71
CONSTANTINOPLE, 61, 71, 73, 77, 81
COPERNICUS, NICOLAUS, **146**
CORNELIA, 29
CORSICA, 2, 21, 168
Courtier, The, 153
CRASSUS, MARCUS LICINIUS, 36
CREMONINI, CESARE, 148
CRIMEAN WAR, 189–90
CRISPI, FRANCESCO, 193–94, 201, 204, 208
CUMAE, 9, 12; helmet, **16–17**

D DACIA, 41, 45, 50
DALMATIA, 45, 58, 73, 205–207
D'ANNUNZIO, GABRIELE, 207
DANTE, 77, **96**, 101–102, 183
DANUBE RIVER, 61, 71, 80
DA PONTE, LORENZO, 160
"DAVID" (Donatello), 113, 116, **117**
"DAVID" (Michelangelo), 131
DE SICA, VITTORIO, 217
DESIDERIUS, 80
Dialogue on the two chief systems of the world, 148–49; title page, **146**
Dialogues concerning two new sciences, 149
DIO CASSIUS, 49
DIOCLETIAN, 55, 58, 60
DIOGENES LAËRTIUS, 49
"DISPUTE ON THE SACRAMENT, THE," 133
Divine Comedy, 101–102
DOMINIC, SAINT, 77
DONATELLO, 113, 116, 120; statue by, **117**
DONATION OF CONSTANTINE,

81, 84
DON GIOVANNI, 160
DUCCIO, painting by, **94**
DUILIUS, consul, 20
DUNANT, JEAN HENRI, 191

E EASTERN ROMAN EMPIRE, 55, 58, 60–61, 72, 77, 80–81, 84
EDUCATION, 41–43, 98, 101, 108–109, 112–13, 116, 147
EDWARD III, of England, 104
EGYPT, 45, 48
ELAGABALUS, 52
EMPEDOCLES, 9
ERASMUS, DESIDERIUS, 152–53
ESTE, ALFONSO I D', 130
ETHIOPIA, **201**, 204, 210–11
ETRUSCANS, 8–10, 12, 15, **16–17**, 17; fresco, **19**; funerary urn, **6**; tomb, **13**

F FABIUS CUNCTATOR, QUINTUS, 23
FALLOPIO, GABRIELLO, 147
FARNESE, ELIZABETH, 159
FASCISM, 207–10, 212–13, 216
FELLINI, FEDERICO, 217
FERDINAND IV, of Naples, 161, 171
FERRARA, 2, 124, 130, 213
FIBONACCI, LEONARDO, 121
FICINI, MARSILIO, 113, 116–19, 121
FILARETE, drawing by, **108–109**
FIUME, 207
FLAMINIUS, GAIUS, 22
FLAVIUS BLONDUS, 130
FLORENCE, 2, 89, 101, 104–27, **126**, 129–30, 140, 143, 150–51; cathedral, **106**; Council of, 119, 121
"FOURTH ESTATE, THE," **202–203**
FRA ANGELICO, 120
FRACASTORO, GIROLAMO, 147
FRANCE, 2, 31, 45, 102, 125–27, 130, 133, 138, 156, 159, 166–79, 183, 186–91, 194–95, 200–201, 205, 210
Francesca da Rimini, 183
FRANCIS I, of France, 135, 138, 152
FRANCIS II, of Sicily, 193, 195, 197
FRANCIS OF ASSISI, SAINT, 77, 95–98, **100**
FRANCO, FRANCISCO, 211
FREDERICK I, Holy Roman Emperor, 95
FREDERICK II, Holy Roman Emperor, 98, 101

G GAIUS, 69

GALBA, 40
GALEN, 147
GALILEO GALILEI, 147–49
GALLA PLACIDIA, 72
GARIBALDI, GIUSEPPE, **184**, 186–87, 190–97, 201, 217
GASPERI, ALCIDE DE, 216
GAUL, 14, 31, 36, 37, 45
GENOA, 2, 88, 168, 175–76, 213
GERMANY, 85, 133, 135, 168, 200, 204–205, 211–13
GETA, PUBLIUS SEPTIMIUS, 47
GHIRLANDAIO, fresco by, **111**
GIANNONE, PIETRO, 160
GIBBON, EDWARD, 168
GIOBERTI, VINCENZO, 184–85, 189
GIORGIONE, 145–47
GIOTTO, 98; painting by, **100**
GOLDONI, CARLO, 159–60
GRACCHI, 29, 32–34
GREAT BRITAIN, 152–53, 166–68, 189–90, 194, 201, 205
GRECO, EL, 153
GREECE, 9–10, 12, 31–32, 45, 49, 72
GREGORY XI, pope, 102–104
GREGORY XIII, pope, 150
GREGORY XVI, pope, 184
GROSLEY, P. J., 169–71
GUARDI, FRANCESCO, 163

HADRIAN, 47–49, 51
HANNIBAL, 21–23, 27, **28**
HARVEY, WILLIAM, 147
HASDRUBAL, 22
HAYDN, FRANZ JOSEPH, 166
"HEALING OF THE DEMONIAC," **136–37**
HENRY III, of France, 142
HENRY VII, Holy Roman Emperor, 102
HENRY VIII, of England, 142
HERCULANEUM, 157, 168
HERODOTUS, 8
History of the Kingdom of Naples, 160
HITLER, ADOLF, 211–12
HOLY ROMAN EMPIRE, 85–105, 155
HONORIUS, FLAVIUS, 72
HORACE, 32, 39
HUMBERT I, of Italy, 204

INDEX, 149, 182
INNOCENT XII, pope, 159
INQUISITION, 140, 149, 152, 157, 182
ITALY, **2**; barbarians, 71–85; city-states, 87–89, 92, 95, 104–105; foreign rule, 155–57, 173–84; geogra-

phy, 7–8, 87; Napoleon and, 173–79; prehistoric, 8–10; Renaissance, 107–56, 160, 163, 173, 217; Risorgimento, 182–97; unification, 197–200. *See also* Roman Empire, Romans, Rome

JEROME, SAINT, 49, **82–83**
JESUITS, 159
JOHN V PALAEOLOGUS, **103**
JOHNSON, SAMUEL, 168
JONES, INIGO, 168
JOSEPH II, Holy Roman Emperor, 157
JUBA II, of Mauretania, 37
JULIUS II, pope, 130–34, 138
JUSTINIAN I, 77
JUVENAL, 43

LADISLAUS, of Naples, 105
LAMPEDUSA, GIUSEPPE DI, 217
LANZA, GIOVANNI, 194
"LAST JUDGMENT, THE," 142, 150
"LAST SUPPER, THE," 124
LATERAN PACT, 210
LAVAL, PIERRE, 210
LAW, 15–17, 32, 34, 41, 49, 66–68, 77, 187
LEAGUE OF NATIONS, 210–11
LEGNANO, 95
LEO X, pope, 125, 133–35
LEOPOLD I, of Tuscany, 157, 163
LEPANTO, 152
LIGURIA, 80, 175–76
LIPPI, FRA FILIPPO, 120
LITERATURE, 16, 159–60, 183–84; ancient, 39, 48–49, 108–109, 112; medieval, 84–85, 101–102; Renaissance, 121, 124, 142
LIUDPRANT, bishop, 84–85
LIVIUS ANDRONICUS, LUCIUS, 16
LIVY, 34, 39, 112
LOMBARDS, 77, 80–81, 84, 173; fibula, **75**
LOMBARDY, 8, 80, 95, 152, 174, 176, 179, 191
LONDON, TREATY OF, 205, 207
LOUIS XIII, of France, 130
LOUIS XIV, of France, 159, 166
LOUIS XV, of France, 168
LOUIS PHILIPPE, 183, 186
LUCRETIA, 18
LUCRETIUS, 109, 119
LUCULLUS, 73
LULLI, GIANBATTISTA, 166
LUTHER, MARTIN, 134–35

LUTHERANISM, 135, 138, 150
LYDIA, 8

M MACHIAVELLI, NICCOLÒ, 52, 127, 129, 133–34, 138, 156, 210
MAMERTINES, 18
MANIN, DANIELE, 186–87, 190
"MAN WITH A GLOVE," 147
MARCELLINUS, SAINT 58
MARCUS AURELIUS, 48–50, 55
MARENGO, 176, **177**
MARIA CAROLINA, of Naples, 174, 176
MARIE ANTOINETTE, 157
MARIUS, GAIUS, 33–36, 110
MARSALA, 193–94
"MARS AND VENUS," **118–19**
MASSACRE OF SAINT BARTHOLOMEW, 150
"MASSACRE OF THE INNOCENTS," **94**
MAXENTIUS, 58–59, **64**
MAXIMIAN, bishop, 71
MAXIMIAN, Roman emperor, 58
MAXIMINUS THE THRACIAN, 52
MAZARIN, JULES, 159
MAZZINI, GIUSEPPE, 182–86, **184**, 189, 191–93, 197
MEDICI, COSIMO DE', **109**, 113, 116, 119–20, 124
MEDICI, COSIMO I DE', 150–51
MEDICI, COSIMO II DE', 148
MEDICI, GIAN GASTONE, 157
MEDICI, LORENZO DE', 116, 120–21, 124–25, 133
MEDICI, PIERO DE' (1414–1469), 120
MEDICI, PIERO DE' (1471–1503), 125
MEDICI FAMILY, 113, 120, 138, 157; bank façade, **108–109**
MEDITERRANEAN SEA, **2**, 7, 21, 22, 23, 31, 45
MESSINA, **2**, 18, 194
MESSINA, STRAIT OF, **2**, 14, 195
METASTASIO, 159
METELLUS, LUCIUS CAECILIUS, 22–23
METTERNICH, PRINCE, 179, 186
MICHELANGELO, 112, 120, 125, 127, 131–34, 142–43, 150
MICHELINO, DOMENICO DI, portrait by, **96**
MICHELOZZO, 113
MILAN, **2**, 8, 59, 88–89, 92, 104, **108–109**, 112–13, 124, 125, 130, 133, 138, 151, 155, 169, 175–76, 186, **188**, 213; cathedral, **172**

MILTIADES, 59–60
MILTON, JOHN, 150, 168
MIRANDOLA, 130
MITHRIDATES VI, 33
MODENA, 130, 179
MONASTICISM, 75–77, **82–83**, 97–98, 169
MONTE CASSINO, 75, 77, 80, 84, 178
MONTEFELTRO, FEDERIGO DA, 124
MONTESQUIEU, BARON DE, 168, 169, 175
MONTEVERDI, CLAUDIO, 166
Moral and Civil Primacy of the Italians, The, 184
MOZART, WOLFGANG AMADEUS, 160
MURAT, JOACHIM, 178
MUSSOLINI, BENITO, 207–13, **209**

N NAPLES, *2*, 104–105, 125, 130, 133, 135, 138, 151–52, 155–57, 169, 173, 176–79, 194–97, 201, **214–15**
NAPOLEON III, of France, 187, 189–91, 193–94
NAPOLEON BONAPARTE, 156, 166, 168, 173–79, **177**, **180–81**
NARSES, general, 77
NERO, 40
NERVI, PIER LUIGI, building by, **198**
NICHOLAS V, pope, 129
NORMANS, 92, 173
NORTH AFRICA, 20, 23, 27, 45, 204, 212
NUMA POMPILIUS, 10, 38

O ODOACER, 73
On Crimes and Punishments, 163
OPERA, 163, 166, 183
Orfeo (Monteverdi), 166
Orfeo (Poliziano), 124
ORVIETO, *2*, 8, **141**
OSTIA, mosaic from, 44
OTHO, MARCUS SALVIUS, 40
OTTO I, emperor, 85
OVID, 40, 120

P PADUA, *2*, 98, 147–48
PAISIELLO, GIOVANNI, 166
PALERMO, *2*, 20, 92, 171, 193–94
PALESTRINA, GIOVANNI, 150
PALLADIO, ANDREA, 143, 153, 168
PAOLI, PASQUALE DI, 168, 173
PAPACY, **78–79**, 80–81, 84–85, 92, 95, 102–105, 125, 129–35, 138, 150–51, 159, 200, 208–10, 213

PAPAL STATES, 84, 98, 102–107, 130, 138–40, 157–59, 174, 178–79, 182–84, 195
PARMA, *2*, 179
PAUL, SAINT, 68
PAUL I, pope, 80
PAUL III, pope, 140
PAUL V, pope, 150
PAUL THE DEACON, 80
PAULUS, AEMILIUS, 27
PAUSANIAS, 49
PAVIA, *2*, 80
PELLICO, SILVIO, 182, 183
PEPIN THE SHORT, 81, 84, 173
PERGOLESI, GIANBATTISTA, 166
PERSANO, CARLO, 197
PERTINAX, 51
PERUGIA, *2*, 8, 130
PHILIP, pope, 81
PHILIP IV, of France, 102
PHILIP V, of Spain, 159
PHILOSTRATUS THE ELDER, 145
PIACENZA, *2*, 135, 179
PIAVE RIVER, 205
PIEDMONT, 156, 174, 176, 179, 186–91, 193–97
PIERO DELLA FRANCESCA, 124
PIRANESI, GIAMBATTISTA, 163; engravings by, **167**
PISA, *2*, 14, 88–89; cathedral, **86**
PIUS II, pope, 119
PIUS V, pope, 151
PIUS VI, pope, 174
PIUS VII, pope, 178
PIUS IX, pope, 184–86
PIUS X, pope, 200, 213
PIUS XI, pope, 216
PLATO, 98, 109, 113, 116, 121, 124, 127, 147–49
PLATONIC ACADEMY, 116–20, 124
PLAUTUS, TITUS MACCIUS, 124
PLINY, 45, 110, 143
POLIZIANO, ANGELO, **111**, 120, 124
POLYBIUS, 22
POMPEII, *2*, 157, **167**, 168; mosaic from, **53**
POMPEY THE GREAT, 36–38
PO RIVER, *2*, 8, 14
PORPORA, NICCOLO, 166
PORSENA, LARS, 10, 12
PRAETORIAN GUARD, 51
Praise of Folly, 153
PRAXITELES, 145
"PRESENTATION OF THE VIRGIN, THE," 145
PRIMATICCIO, FRANCESCO, 152
"PRIMAVERA," 120
Prince, The, 129, 133, 138, 210
PRISCILLA CATACOMB, 67

PTOLEMY, 146
PUNIC WARS: First, 18–21, 22; Second, 21–23, 27, **28**, 29
PYTHAGORAS, 9, 10

R RADETZKY, JOSEPH, 186
RAPHAEL, 133–34; painting by, **139**
RATCHIS, 80
RAVENNA, *2*, 72–74, 77, 80–81, 84, 92; San Vitale, 70, 77
RAYMOND, SAINT, **139**
REGULUS, MARCUS ATILIUS, 20
RELIGION, ancient, 12, 17, **19**, 29, **35**, 43, 52, **60**, 72. See *also* Christianity
REMUS, 10, **21**
RENAISSANCE, 107–53, 155–56, 160, 163, 173, 217
REVOLUTION, FRENCH, 171–74
RIENZI, COLA DI, 92
RISO, FRANCESCO, 193
RISORGIMENTO, 182–97
ROGER II, of Sicily, 92
ROMAN CATHOLIC CHURCH, 68, 92, 95, 119, 127, 133–35, 140, 149–50, 184–86, 200, 208–11, 213, 216
ROMAN EMPIRE, 39–45, 47–69, 71; equipage, **38**
ROMANS, 10–18, 22–23, 27–29, 32–33, 40–45, 49–50, 66–69, 110, 112, 130–31, 140; chariot race, **56–57**; gladiators, 43, **62**; principate, 39–55; Punic Wars, 18–23, 27, **28**, 29; Republic, 31–38, 87, 130, 168; triumvirate, 36–38; war machine, **16–17**
ROME, *2*, 10–17, 29, 33–34, 38–48, 50, 58–61, 66, 72, 80–81, 84, 92, 104–105, 127–35, 138–42, 147–50, **158**, 163, **167**, 169, 171, 178–79, 182, 186–87, 194–95, 200, 208, **209**, 212; Café Greco, **190**; Colosseum, **30**, 43, 129; Forum, **42**, 129; Palatine hill, 10, **24–25**, 39
ROMULUS, 10, **21**
ROMULUS AUGUSTULUS, 73
ROSSELLINI, ROBERTO, 217
ROSSINI, GIOACCHINO ANTONIO, 183
ROSSO, IL, 152
"ROUT OF SAN ROMANO," **114–15**
RUBICON RIVER, 37

S SABINES, 14–15
SADOLETO, JACOPO, 133

"SAINT MARY THE EGYPTIAN," 147
SAINT PETER'S BASILICA, 65, 131, 133–34, **158**, 163; interior, **128**
SAN GIMIGNANO, **99**
SANSOVINO, JACOPO, 142–43
SARACENS, 87, 92
SARDINIA, 2, 7, 8, 21, 155–57, 163, 174, 179
SARPI, PAOLO, 150
SAVONAROLA, GIROLAMO, 124–27, **126**
SAVOY, 190–91
SAXA RUBRA, 59
SCAEVOLA, GAIUS MUCIUS, 10, 12, 18
SCARLATTI, ALESSANDRO, 166
"SCHOOL OF ATHENS," 133
SCIPIO AFRICANUS, PUBLIUS CORNELIUS, 23, **26**, 27, 29, 32, 110
SCULPTURE, 63–65, 113, 116, 120, 131
SEVERUS, LUCIUS SEPTIMIUS, 51; arch of, **46**
SEVERUS, MARCUS AURELIUS ALEXANDER, 52
SFORZA, LODOVICO, 124
SICILY, 2, 7–8, 18, 20–23, 84, 92, 152, 155, 193–97, 201, 212, 216–17
SIDNEY, SIR PHILIP, 153
SIENA, fresco from, **90–91**
SIGISMUND, emperor, 104
SIXTUS IV, pope, 116, 129
"SLEEPING VENUS," 145–47
SOCIALISM 200–201, 204, 207–208, 213, 216
SOCRATES, 110, 112, 118
SOLFERINO, 191
SPAIN, 23, 130, 133, 135, 138, 140, 149–56, 179, 211
SPALLANZANI, LAZZARO, 175
"SQUARE OF SAINT MARK'S, THE," **164–65**
STEPHEN II, pope, 81
STEPHEN III, pope, 81
STILICHO, FLAVIUS, 72
STURZO, LUIGI, 213, 216
SUETONIUS, 36–37, 40
SULLA, LUCIUS CORNELIUS, 33–34, 36
Summa theologica, 98
SYLVESTER I, pope, 81

T TACITUS, CORNELIUS, 34
TANUCCI, BERNARDO DI, 157
TARQUINII, 2, 10
TARQUINIUS SUPERBUS, LUCIUS, 10, 18, 23
TETZEL, JOHANN, 134
THEODORA, 77
THEODORIC, 73–74
THEODOSIUS I, 61

THOMAS AQUINAS, SAINT, 98, 101
TIBERIUS, 40
TIEPOLO, GIANBATTISTA, 163
TINTORETTO, JACOPO, 145–47, 153
TITIAN, 143, 145–47, 152
TITUS, 43
TOSCANELLI, PAOLO, 120
TRAJAN, 40–41, 45–47, 50, 69
Treatise on the Interdict, 150
TRENT, COUNCIL OF, 150
TRIESTE, 2, 205
TRISSINO, GIANGIORGIO, 143
TUNISIA, 2, 200
TUSCANY, 8–9, 15, 22, 80, **90–91**, 99, 148, 156–57, 178–79, 191

U UCCELLO, PAOLO, 120; painting by, **114–15**
UMBRIA, 195, 197
URBAN VI, pope, 104
UTRECHT, PEACE OF, 155

V VALENS, 61
VALERIAN, 52
VASI, engraving by, **170**
VATICAN, 133, 135, 200; Gallery of Geographical Maps, **154**; Sistine Chapel, 129, 131, 134, 142
VENICE, 2, 88–89, 104, 113, 130, **136–37**, 140–50, **144**, 151, 152, 155–56, 163, **164–65**, 166, 169, 171, 174, 186–87, 194; Republic, 140, 143, 205
VERDI, GIUSEPPE, 183
VERONA, 2, 89, 213
VERONESE, PAOLO, 143–45
VERSAILLES PEACE TALKS, 205
VESALIUS, ANDREAS, 147
VESPUCCI, AMERIGO, 121
VICO, GIAN BATTISTA, 160
VICTOR EMMANUEL II, of Italy, **185**, 186, 189, 193–97, 200, 208
VIENNA, CONGRESS OF, 179
VILLA ADRIANA, **50**
VILLAFRANCA, 191
VILLANOVAN CULTURE, urn, **6**
VILLARI, PASQUALE, 81
VINCI, LEONARDO DA, 112, 124, 152, 176; drawings by, **122–23**
VISCONTI, GIAN GALEAZZO, 104–105, 112
VISCONTI, LUCHINO, 217
VISCONTI FAMILY, 88, 104; emblem, **93**
VITELLIUS, AULIUS, 40
VITRUVIUS, 113, 143
VOLTURNO RIVER, 2, 195, 197

W WESTERN SCHISM, 104–105
WILLIAM I, of England, 89
WILSON, WOODROW, 205
WINCKELMANN, JOHANN, 168
WORLD WAR I, 204–205
WORLD WAR II, 211–13

Y YUGOSLAVIA, 2, 205–207

Z ZOG I, of Albania, 211